COMMONSENSE
BUSINESS
IN A
NONSENSE
ECONOMY

COMMONSENSE BUSINESS IN A NONSENSE ECONOMY

The Entrepreneur's Guide to Avoiding Pitfalls and Maximizing Assets—in Good Times and Bad

Steven R. Gottry

Amsterdam • Johannesburg • Oxford
San Diego • Sydney • Toronto

This publication is designed to provide accurate and authoritative information in regard to the subject matter covered. It is sold with the understanding that the publisher is not engaged in rendering legal, accounting, or other professional service. If legal advice or other expert assistance is required, the services of a competent professional person should be sought. *From a Declaration of Principles jointly adopted by a Committee of the American Bar Association and a Committee of Publishers.*

Editor: Jackie Estrada
Production Editor: Katharine Pechtimaldjian
Editorial Assistant: Susan Rachmeler
Page Compositor: Susan Odelson
Cover Design: Eric Walljasper

Library of Congress Cataloging-in-Publication Data
Gottry, Steven R.
    Commonsense business in a nonsense economy: the entrepreneur's guide to avoiding pitfalls and maximizing assets—in good times and bad / Steven R. Gottry.
      p. cm.
Includes bibliographical references and index.
ISBN 0-89384-259-1 (pbk.)
    1. New business enterprises—United States. 2. Entrepreneurship—United States. 3. Small business—United States. I. Title.
HD62.5.G677   1994   94-5601
658.4'21—dc20   CIP

Printed in the United States of America.
Printing 1 2 3 4 5 6 7 8 9 10

DEDICATION

The lessons in this book come as the result not only of being in business for myself, but also as one of the many benefits of my marriage.

A marriage is, in part, a small business. Every married couple must create a legal partnership, locate a "facility" in which to "set up shop," and manage cash flow, payables, and investments to maximize return.

As children join the firm, there are personnel issues to resolve, and facilities expansion matters to evaluate.

Ultimately, the disposition of the company's assets enters into consideration.

I am fortunate to have a first-rate marriage partner, Karla Styer Gottry, to whom I dedicate this book. Knowing that writing this was important to me, she packed me up and sent me alone on a trip to the warm sunshine of Palm Springs, California, to write. When the Minnesota summer finally arrived, she encouraged me to spend several "writing weekends" at a small A-frame cabin in the woods of Wisconsin. That's sacrifice!

Without Karla's support, patience, and understanding, this book would have remained nothing more than an idea lodged somewhere in the back of my mind. Thank you!

CONTENTS

ACKNOWLEDGMENTS

I have benefited from the friendship of, and advice and mentoring from, a number of people over the years. It would be impossible to thank them all, but several deserve a special mention.

My parents, Roger and Helen Gottry, taught me the value of independent thinking and provided sound moral teaching. And from my wonderful children, Jonathan, Michelle, and Kalla Paige, I have discovered the rewards of instilling those values in the next generation.

My high school teachers, particularly Jerry Beckman, Dorothy Tweet, Ole Loing, and Douglas Degree, all believed that encouragement and personal involvement are an integral part of education. College professors who had an immeasurable influence on my career path include Jack Mark, and the late—and always beloved—Harold Wilson and Leonard Bart, all of the University of Minnesota.

My business support group deserves my special thanks: Dudley Ryan, my CPA; Jim Gilbert, my attorney; Steve Kalin, my insurance and estate planner; and Dan Gottry, my younger brother and an involved board member. All have contributed substantial guidance over the years. Thanks, too, to my staff—past, present, and future— for letting me test my theories and principles on them.

During some difficult periods of business, I received invaluable support and advice from Richard Young, of Bayfields, Inc., and Chuck Wanous, president of Kerker & Associates, an advertising agency that at one time faced a situation similar to mine.

Clients and friends who deserve my gratitude are Clint Miller of The Shelard Group/ONCOR International;

Ryan Toole of Prudential Realty Group (and Ryan's wife Carolyn); Chuck "Comeback" Wenger; good friends Pam ("Always-There-for-Me") Benoit and her husband, Gary; Tony and Dawn Dempsey; Jim and Lynne McDonald; Ric Jacobsen; Harriet Crosby; Bill and Joan Brown; and especially Richard Baltzell, formerly of Revell Publishing, who has lent his encouragement and invaluable assistance to this project.

It would be impossible to overlook Duane Pederson, who gave me some tremendous opportunities to express my creativity while I was yet in high school (and who today devotes his life to befriending the homeless, the poor, runaway teens, and the imprisoned); Tom Cousins, former promotion director of WCCO-TV; and Thomas H. Tipton, founder of Vanguard Advertising, the first black-owned advertising agency in Minnesota (the third in the United States), and now a renowned gospel singer and unfailing friend.

During life's toughest moments, my personal faith has been a source of immeasurable strength. Mark Darling, Brent Knox, and the staff and people of Evergreen Community Church in Bloomington, Minnesota, along with my fellow Rotarian, Father Dick Smith, have helped me better understand that, through faith, I don't have to fight my battles alone. Thank you!

Thanks to my editor, Jackie Estrada, who tightened things up while retaining the emphasis I wanted, and who helped improve the book's flow and clarity.

Perhaps my most unusual acknowledgments are John Sculley, Steve Jobs, and Steve Wozniak, the powers behind the Macintosh PowerBook notebook computer (I don't leave home without it!), and Bill Gates (an entrepreneur of larger-than-life proportions), whose Microsoft Word 5.1— together with the computer—helped make this work possible.

PREFACE

In the business sense, I believe there are just four basic types of people:

1. Those who have started their own businesses. These are people who have acted on their dreams. They have an entrepreneurial spirit and the desire to be their own bosses. They want to exercise some control over their own destinies.

2. Those who *want* to own a business and become their own bosses. Their ambitions, however, are limited by something that to them seems insurmountable. Perhaps they believe they don't have access to the necessary financial resources. Perhaps they are secure and comfortable in their jobs and feel they can't afford to take the risk. Maybe their dreams aren't backed by sufficient drive. Possibly they're stalled by fear.

3. Those who have started companies sometime in the past, only to see them fail. The death of a business is one of the most painful things an owner can ever witness.

4. Those who have no interest in owning their own business. They want the perceived security and stability (at least in good economic times) of working for someone else. They can't imagine the joys and joyous tribulations that accompany business ownership. They are limited because their dreams are limited.

This book is written for the first group of people. But it's also written for the second group, to help them explore the possibilities of business ownership as seen from the perspective of someone who has been there. And it's written for the third group, because, if they still possess the entrepreneurial spirit, they may be considering a second start-up or a new business; this book will help them take more of the necessary basics into account.

The last group probably won't see this book. Nevertheless, if they *were* to read it, they would gain some insights into the struggles their employers face. They would realize that their bosses aren't necessarily in the enviable positions they thought they were.

Another group who will probably never see this book are the M.B.A.'s—the people who understand and preach the research-driven concepts and mathematical formulas that make sense in a master's thesis but have little application on the battleground of small business. You will quickly see that this book contains no business theory, no statistical analyses, no accounting procedures, no investment strategies, and no observations on international banking and global monetary systems. These things have little relation to my day-to-day life, although I'm sure someone out there could argue that I would be more successful if I had paid more attention to them.

This book is clearly written from the perspective of a "typical" small business owner. I operate neither the most successful nor the most stable business around. But I have confronted most of the questions and faced most of the problems that are common to small business. And I have been able to attach enough correct solutions to those questions and problems to remain in business for twenty-three years—through at least three or four recessions (depending on how a recession is defined), and through almost unbelievable ups and downs.

If there is but one nugget of wisdom in this book that helps your business—or your future business—prosper, I will have felt that I accomplished something useful.

INTRODUCTION

I have already been where you are—or where you may hope to be. I have lived many of the dreams every entrepreneur shares. And I have seen them nearly die. I have had my successes and my failures. I have been the envy of my peers. I have gone back to my fifteenth, and twentieth, and twenty-fifth high school reunions as the success my classmates never thought I would be.

True, I have never been among the ranks of the H. Ross Perots, the Curt Carlsons, the Donald Trumps, the Ted Turners, or the Lee Iacoccas. You've never seen my name in *Forbes* or *Fortune*—or even *People*.

But I have enjoyed a degree of success, at least as measured by the material standards that many people choose to use.

I have owned six Mercedes-Benz automobiles over a seventeen-year period. The world was almost perfect when viewed through a gold-plated three-pointed Mercedes star. I sat on leather seats and pushed buttons that adjusted those seats to the perfect driving position by memory. I listened to my choice of music on exotic stereo systems. I glided along on pitted freeways and pot-holed side streets, oblivious to the bumps that those in lesser cars were experiencing.

But not today.

I learned how to fly in my own airplane. I earned my instrument rating in my second airplane—an impressive high-performance little hummer with retractable gear and all the bells and whistles I had always wanted, from (forgive me, nonpilots) digital VOR and communications radios to Loran C navigation, autopilot, thunderstorm detection, and distance-measuring equipment—the stuff of an aviator's dreams. As I traveled to my business destination, I listened to music over my stereo intercom system.

But not today.

I took up boating in 1975. It seemed like a pleasant diversion. I started out with a 15-footer with an outboard motor. I moved up to a 22-foot inboard/outboard. Then a 26-foot cruiser with a complete galley, two cabins, and a bathroom (head, for you boaters) with a shower. Next came the 30-footer with dual steering stations, twin engines, and a fly-bridge that offered a panoramic view of my domain, beautiful Lake Minnetonka. Every few years, I traded for bigger and better.

But not today.

When I wanted to impress a client with an evening out on the town, I would phone the livery service that managed my stretch limousine and book it—along with a chauffeur in a tuxedo. As we headed toward one of the better restaurants or clubs in town, we'd watch a video on the color TV, listen to the stereo, or make phone calls to those fine restaurants and clubs to confirm our reservations. Or maybe we'd just buzz the chauffeur on the intercom to chat.

But not today.

If I wanted a new television, I'd choose one with a 45-inch picture. Or one that projected a 100-inch picture on the wall. A new stereo had to be an exotic Danish model—a Bang & Olufsen. When I bought a new sofa—for office or home—it had to be covered in leather. All of my attaché cases and travel bags were made of Canadian belting leather by Hartmann. My pens were Montblanc. Every new camera I purchased was a Hasselblad, a top-of-the-line Nikon, or the best Sony camcorder on the market.

But not today.

I spent my vacations with my wife and children in Hawaii, Mexico, Aruba, the Bahamas, and Disneyland. I cruised the Caribbean on five different cruise ships. I golfed with high-powered executives at exclusive country clubs and dined with senators and members of Congress, governors and mayors.

But not today.

By now, you *have* to be asking, "What happened to this guy, and why am I wasting my time reading his book?"

What happened to me is that I made nonsense business decisions during the "fat" business years, and didn't respond quickly enough to problems in the "lean" years. And I paid the price for my mistakes.

Why you should read this book is to avoid the same mistakes. And to gain a few—or many—insights into running a successful business, so that yours can prosper in both good times and bad.

I know the statement that follows will sound like bragging, but *I wish I could have been able to read my own book ten or fifteen years ago.* The truth is that many of the business books on the shelves today offer a lot of wonderful-sounding theory, but they have little practical application in the real world of small business. This book is full of life-and-death ideas, developed in the trenches.

Is this book profound? Absolutely not! It is a very basic compilation of commonsense ideas. If I had known, understood, and applied the principles in this book throughout my business life, I quite possibly would not have gone through all the struggles and changes that stripped me of the material trappings of success.

But you should know that, as you read these words, I am a greater success than I have ever been. I am happy, content, and fulfilled. I am rich beyond description. My riches are my wife and children. My family. My friends who have stood by me through every twist and turn in life's pathway. My values and beliefs. And my firm conviction that circumstances do not have to control my actions, hopes, and dreams.

I am successful because I am keeping my word, fulfilling my promises, forgiving those who have let me down, paying off my debt, and rebuilding my life with confidence. I am charting a new and exciting course for my business, and I am using my own writings as my guide!

The nasty bumps and turns in the economy can devastate my business and take my money, but they can't take away who I am or what I believe. They can't strip me of hope or erase my dreams.

Will I drive another Mercedes? Yes, if it makes business sense.

Will I own another airplane? Only if that, too, makes business sense.

Will I buy a bigger boat? Hey, doesn't everyone dream of a 100-foot yacht?

Will I once again vacation in Hawaii, cruise the Caribbean, play golf with high-powered business executives and dine with senators? Yes! *Absolutely!* These things *do* make business sense! Vacations are an essential time-out from the pressures of business. And my business's future depends on the decisions of high-powered executives and government officials.

So, join me, please, on that roller coaster ride in "amusement park hell" called small business. Follow me through the various stages of the business life cycle. Learn from my mistakes. Become stronger, more focused, more successful. Discover how to be *positive* even in a negative business climate.

Begin with me where we all begin in business—at square one.

PART ONE

The Small-Business Life Cycle

1

THE DREAMING STAGE

I have a great appreciation for any news article, short story, speech, or book in which the first sentence grabs me. *The Great Gatsby*, by F. Scott Fitzgerald, is such a book. When I first picked it up, I read these words: "In my younger and more vulnerable years my father gave me some advice that I've been turning over in my mind ever since. 'Whenever you feel like criticizing anyone,' he told me, 'just remember that all the people in this world haven't had the advantages that you've had.' " Those words begin a novel that portrays the fears, agonies, and misdirected desires experienced by two distinct groups of people: the poor and the rich.

In reading and reflecting on Fitzgerald's words, it seemed to me at the time that if we are all born to the doubts, loneliness, and pain of the human experience, it is better to be one of the rich ones than one of the poor ones. Besides, coming from a modest home in a small farming town in southwestern Minnesota, I had never *seen* wealth, let alone experienced it, and I thought it might be worth a try.

As a caring, giving person—thanks to my upbringing—I knew that I didn't want money just for myself and my own selfish goals. I wanted it for the rest of the people for whom I could create a better life: My family. Worthy charities. The starving people in China my mother brought

---

up every time I didn't want to clean my plate. The nearest Mercedes dealer.

Fortunately, I had learned something crucial from watching my father, my grandfathers, and the employed fathers and mothers of my high school friends. Most people do not get rich as the result of working for others.

After considerable thought about the matter, I concluded that there are only seven ways to gain great wealth:

1. Win some form of lottery or magazine publisher's sweepstakes. (When I was younger, the equivalent of the lottery was television game shows such as *The $64,000 Question.*)

2. Develop an idea that can be franchised. (Another McDonald's would be the ticket!)

3. Invent something that everyone needs, preferably on a repeat basis. (I've heard that the person who invented those little plastic whatevers on the ends of shoelaces retired in utter opulence.)

4. Become a movie, television, recording, or sports star.

5. Invest in stocks, bonds, buildings, and land—but only in those that are absolutely guaranteed to increase in value.

6. Inherit—or marry into—big bucks.

7. Start a business, devote a tremendous amount of energy to it, and make it prosper and grow.

Great ideas, one and all. But on further thought, I ruled out the first six methods. The odds against winning some form of lottery are astronomical, in spite of the widely held belief that "*someone* has to win it—might as well be me."

As to the others?

I'm no Ray Kroc of McDonald's, and besides, the world probably doesn't need another fast-food chain. Although if there were a drive-through sushi bar in my neighborhood, I'd be a regular.

I don't have a mechanical mind.

I can't act, sing, or dance, and I was always chosen last for every sport or game.

Nearly every stock I've ever purchased has declined in value. (Almost half of the companies in which I have invested are out of business. Ever hear of Fingermatrix or New World Computer? I didn't think so.)

And I don't have any wealthy relatives or friends. (I know a fellow about my age who, for years, has actually befriended elderly wealthy people in the hope that they will put him in their wills. That's unbelievably tacky, but I'm pleased to report that it hasn't worked for him—yet.)

As you can see, the only option that remains for us hard working, highly motivated, but otherwise average people is to start a business and nurture it to growth and profitability.

For many years, when my wife, Karla, and I would talk at the end of a long day at the office or on the road, she would ask jokingly, "Are we rich yet?"

Today's answer, of course, would be "No." Not in terms of material goodies, at least. But even with the recent downs we've experienced, we're a long way from where we started more than twenty-four years ago. I'm a long way from the small house with linoleum floors and asbestos siding in the small farming town where I grew up. I'm a long way from the late-night hours of pumping gas and doing oil changes and grease jobs to earn money for college. (I still pump gas, but I only pump it into my car—at three or four times the price it was back then.)

These days—very honestly—accumulating money is not my primary goal. Any money I do make is simply the result of providing a useful service at a fair price—and being in demand as a result. During my first several years in business, though, I thought of myself as virtually unstoppable. I was on the fast track to big bucks. I have since been taught that money is one of the more temporal things in life. Throughout history, fortunes have been lost as quickly as they have been made.

The Business Climate

Just as *The Great Gatsby* grabbed my attention from the first line, so did *A Tale of Two Cities* by Charles Dickens, the classic novel that begins with the words: "It was the best of times. It was the worst of times."

That fairly well describes a day in the life of the small businessperson. But it also describes something of a grander scale: the peaks and valleys of the economy in which every business must function—and strive to be profitable.

It's no secret that the U.S. economy is out of control. The simple, obvious, and ever-present truth is that the people we have elected to govern us spend more money than they collect through the taxes they impose on us. Not just occasionally, but every day. The result of such irresponsibility is inevitably recession, inflation, higher taxation, or a combination of the three. Which of those alternatives would you prefer?

If you need a clearer picture of the huge mess we've created for ourselves, read one of the current "hazards of deficit spending" books on the market, such as *The Coming Economic Earthquake* by Larry Burkett.[1] While you may view some of what the author says with skepticism, there is probably enough solid fact in his book to motivate you to become more involved in the complex workings of the political process. We need to elect fiscally responsible individuals to public office at every level of government.

If you own a small business and you survived the recession, congratulations! You're one of the lucky ones. But you may not be so fortunate the next time around. According to Burkett and others, the evidence points to a deeper, longer, more severe downturn the next time the cycle plays out. And when it's deeper, longer, and more severe, it's not called a recession. It's a depression—1930s style. There are, I believe, even tougher days for businesses—and workers and families—ahead.

That's the bad news. The good news is that there will always be a place—in virtually any economy—for well-run businesses that provide meaningful and necessary products or services at competitive prices. And they will always provide jobs for others.

Your business—existing now or in your future plans—could be among them. But only if you play it smart. You must know what to do in both good times and bad. You must be prepared to make tough but logical decisions. You must understand where you are in the business life cycle and use that knowledge to your advantage.

Recession is the ultimate judge and jury for both companies and employees. Recession weeds out unproductive people and nonproducing companies. (In the most severe cases, it also weeds productive people out of unproductive companies, an unfortunate miscarriage of justice.)

Recession is often a swift judge. At other times, it is slow and deliberate. Its speed depends on the "crimes" of the business's owner or managers. Are the crimes intentional or accidental? Is the effect of poor management immediate or cumulative? Are the crimes honest mistakes or deliberate deceptions?

Among other things, this book is designed to keep you honest. Its purpose is to prevent you from committing the common business "crimes" that could ultimately lead to the harshest of sentences: business failure.

I have been forced, through the ravages of recession, to apply many of the principles I write about—quickly and almost heartlessly. As you read this, you can be sure that I will have undergone many additional changes. But I can promise you two things: I will be in *some* kind of business, and it will be successful!

It Begins With a Dream

"What makes you qualified to write a book on business?" I have been asked. "Do you have a degree in business? Are you a Harvard M.B.A?"

Well, no, actually. My lowly B.A. degrees are in advertising (School of Journalism) and radio-television production (School of Speech, Communications, and Theater Arts) from the University of Minnesota. Since that time, I have toyed with the idea of enrolling in law school. To date, though, my postgraduate education consists of a private pilot's license, an instrument rating in airplanes, a few seminars that have barely kept me awake, and a lot of reading. A *lot* of reading.

Two simple factors qualify me to write this book.

First, I began my business on graduation from college in 1970, have operated it continuously since that time, and have experienced growth in both gross revenues and gross profits in every year but one. I know I won't see growth in revenues this year, but thanks to the self-analysis that led to this book, I will see a growth in profits. And profits, ultimately, are "where it's at" for business.

Second, I have probably made more business mistakes than any person alive, but I have learned from my mistakes, taken notes on them, and applied what I have learned as best I can.

Am I another H. Ross Perot, who started a business for $1,000 and sold it for $2.5 billion? No. Will I ever be another H. Ross Perot? Probably not—so I won't be able to afford to run for president of the United States.

I am in the same category as the vast majority of other small businesspeople. I own a company that provides me with an income and that provides good jobs for a handful of other people. Over the years, my company has grown steadily, but not spectacularly. My primary business is The Gottry Communications Group, Inc., a mix of an advertising/marketing firm, a video production facility, and a newsletter development entity.

My company began as a dream when I was in high school, in that small farming town in southwestern Minnesota. Throughout high school, I was something of a promoter. I earned my commercial radio operator's license at age fourteen, and by sixteen, I had talked my way into a job as a disc jockey at the local radio station. I sponsored concerts by touring musical groups and promoted everything from school plays to the Red Cross bloodmobile.

When my senior year social studies teacher assigned a term paper on personal career choices, I knew exactly what I was going to write about. I wanted to start my own advertising/public relations business. That was my dream. And nearly three decades later, that term paper is still filed in the lower right-hand drawer of my desk. (Yes, I *did* get an A on it.)

From my first day at the University of Minnesota in September 1965, I knew what my majors would be. I worked my way through college—with as much help as my parents could give me—as a hospital orderly, a freelance designer and wedding photographer, and a "go-fer" in the promotion department of the local CBS television affiliate. I graduated without honors, and without debt.

A few weeks before commencement exercises, my graphic design professor confirmed what I had already decided. He said, "Of all the students I've had over the years, you're the only one I have ever advised to hang out his own shingle." That's all I needed to hear!

In spite of the need to pay for most of the costs of my education, I had managed to save about $125 through my freelance design work. That seemed like plenty of money on which to start an advertising agency, but my lawyer at the time—a wonderful elderly gentleman who offered to handle the incorporation process for me if I simply paid his out-of-pocket expenses—didn't seem to agree. He pointed out that in the state of Minnesota, $1,000 was the minimum capital investment required for incorporation. "Well, I have other assets besides cash," I told him. "I have a well-worn IBM electric typewriter that my father bought for me. I have a four-drawer file cabinet, a drawing board and a T-square, and a nearly antique manual adding machine. Why, the typewriter alone has appreciated dramatically over the past several years, to the point where I'm sure it's worth at least a thousand dollars!" With a sly little wink he agreed, and I became an "Inc." My dream was marching toward reality.

All dreams, though, need a foundation of reality. You must have a deep personal interest in the business you are contemplating, as well as training in and knowledge of the field. Your dreams must be based on a measure of research.

You need to know whether you have a reasonable chance for success.

If your dream is to open a sushi bar in a small Missouri town of 1,200 residents, you're probably doomed to fail. If you plan to set up a bait and tackle store in west Texas, 150 miles from the nearest good fishing lake or stream, good luck! And if your dream is to operate a video rental store in a strip mall that already has three video rental stores, you may find the going pretty slow.

The FANAFI Principle

The secret to small-business success is something I refer to as FANAFI. It's the acronym for the old saying "Find a Need and Fill It."

If you want to start a business to fill a need that no longer exists (horse-drawn carriage repair, for example), that has not grown sufficiently to assure your profitability (laserdisc rentals, as opposed to videotape rentals), or that only the strongest of economies will support (selling only $1,000-and-up vacuum cleaners), you're not taking the FANAFI principle into consideration.

Take a moment to reflect on needs that have recently come to the forefront and the businesses that have been formed to fill those needs.

The availability of inexpensive home VCRs has led to the birth and growth of video rental outlets and VCR repair services.

The time crunch that most people face, coupled with their impatience and unwillingness to wait in lines, has resulted in a number of services designed to save time and effort: the 20-minute-or-less oil change facility; one-hour photo processing labs; pizza delivery services; fast-food restaurant drive-throughs; instant cash machines (automated tellers).

New needs, new technologies, and new generations of consumers will lead to a multitude of new business opportunities. The businesses that succeed will be those that fulfill a genuine need for a large enough market—and that are well run.

As you dream, make certain those dreams mesh with reality, and you will have a good shot at success.

2

THE PLANNING STAGE

My friend Jack Liemandt, now in his eighties, started a small clothing business nearly fifty years ago. He grew the business into a chain of men's clothing stores that was so successful it eventually attracted the attention of Hart, Schaffner, & Marx, which offered Jack a tidy sum for the chain. (Most of us dream of a similar scenario!)

Jack recently told me that his business career has been guided by a simple, straightforward principle found in the ancient book of Proverbs: "Any enterprise is built by wise planning, becomes strong through common sense, and profits wonderfully by keeping abreast of the facts."

This little nugget of truth should be incredibly obvious to everyone in business. A multitude of costly mistakes and disastrous business failures could be avoided if entrepreneurs paid attention to its three components: wise planning, common sense, and up-to-date information.

I started making critical mistakes from the day I opened the doors of my business. The first was that I had no business plan. No five-year plan. No three-year plan. No one-year plan. Not even a one-month plan. In fact, I had no plan for the next day.

All I knew for sure was that my brand-new ad agency had one client, and that client had promised two months' work in the form of one project. Although I was fortunate in that one order was all I needed to get started, that's not usually a strong enough basis to get a business up and running and keep it going.

After you've dreamed your dreams, you have to plan your plan. A good initial plan takes several factors into account. You have to ask—and answer—the basic what, when, where, who, and how questions. Just as a news reporter asks these kinds of questions to establish the facts behind a fast-breaking story, you have to ask them to establish the direction of your business.

1. *When* are you going to start your business?
2. *Where* are you going to start it?
3. *What* are you going to name it?
4. *How* are you going to position it?
5. *How* are you going to determine your investment needs and finance them?
6. *What kind* of business structure are you going to establish? Sole proprietorship, partnership, or corporation?
7. *How many* employees will you need, and what do they have to accomplish?
8. *What policies* will apply to those employees?

These questions are so simple, so fundamental. Yet it's surprising how many small businesspersons overlook one or more of them.

All of these questions demand answers. Every facet of these issues must be written down, evaluated, and discussed with trusted advisers.

Let me be one of your advisers and share some thoughts on each of these questions.

When Are You Going to Start Your Business?

The obvious answer is, "When the time is right—when the cosmic forces of concept and financing come together." That's almost correct.

The correct answer is, "When there is a *valid need* that someone can fulfill at a profit, and *you* are in the best position—by virtue of interest, expertise, and financial capability—to meet it." The hope is that you'll be in the best position to meet that need *ahead* of everyone else. Late entrants usually have a tougher go of it, unless they can come up with a new slant, can offer better pricing, or can out-market the competition.

This answer presupposes a number of things. Enough residents of west Texas have to *need* and *want* a local bait shop, even if there's no fishing within miles. Every person in that Missouri town of 1,200 has to crave sushi three or four days a week. I can't overemphasize that your planning must begin with the FANAFI principle.

If you are considering leaving your current job, no matter what it is or how much you are paid, you must be in a position to accept a major reduction in income for the first several weeks, months, and possibly even years, when you start your own business. If you can't do that, you can't answer the question "When?" and you should probably pass this book along to a more courageous friend.

In 1970, I was offered a full-time, likely-secure job in the advertising department of our local phone company. It paid $9,800 per year to start. Today, those would be virtually poverty-level wages. But back then, it was a fairly enticing offer, especially for a college student who had been making $1.90 an hour at a part-time job.

I said "Sorry, no thanks," and struck out on my own. During the first few months, while fulfilling the terms of my initial contract with my first client, I had taken on some additional assignments, and I was actually making what amounted to the monthly equivalent of the $9,800 annual income I had been offered by Ma Bell.

Then I hit my first dry spell. I experienced my first bad receivable, along with a reduction in work orders. Just five months before my first child was due, my gross income was $60—for the *entire* month. Four months before his birth, it increased to the whopping sum of $75.

I had traded a sure thing—a job with the phone company—for an unsure thing: my own business. And for some strange, undefinable, entrepreneurial reason, I loved it!

It was difficult. It still is. The tough times have been mixed in with the good times. But the good times always seem to win out—even when I'm locked in a battle with the nonsense economy.

Where Are You Going to Start It?

Every real estate broker can quote the oldest axiom on the books: "The three most important things about real estate are *location, location, location.*"

When it comes to most new businesses, location is only one of several important considerations. But it's still vital.

As you investigate a prospective location, look at the neighborhood. Is the population sufficient to support your business? Are the demographics—age, income, gender—a good match for your business? You won't sell much baby furniture in a retirement community.

Is the neighborhood clean, safe, and inviting, or is it deteriorating? Are other businesses in the area successful?

Next, consider traffic counts. If most of the traffic sticks to a main artery three blocks north of your proposed location, better think again. When your business is one that relies on high traffic to be successful, you must be situated on a well-traveled street.

Make sure you have good access, especially if you're planning to locate along a freeway or major highway. All roads may lead to you, but do all exits?

In a suburb of Minneapolis, a beautiful restaurant facility sits on a service road adjacent to a major highway. Five or six unique and interesting restaurants have occupied that building. All of them have failed. The building has great visibility, but it has one problem. You can only get to it when you're going eastbound, toward downtown. There's no nearby exit when you're headed west on your way home. And if you leave home and drive east to go there, you have to go further east when you leave before you can turn around.

Next, carefully consider the prospects for growth in the area. Are people building new homes? Are apartment buildings going up? Is vacant land being developed into malls and office parks? If there are a lot of "for lease or sale" signs in the windows, find out why. Chances are, the businesses have failed because of the location.

If you're setting up a manufacturing or distribution operation, naturally you'll have to look at all aspects of area services, zoning, rail spur access, roads that can handle trucking loads, availability of a good labor pool, and so on—issues too varied and complex to explore here.

Avoid the temptation to take the second-best location based on lower lease rates. Where you open your business has a tremendous impact on whether you will succeed.

What Are You Going to Name It?

Think carefully about the name you plan to give your business. Some names simply don't work. Try these:

CRASH HARD DRIVES. It's what every computer owner or operator dreads.

HOOKER'S THERAPEUTIC MASSAGE. Sounds like they'll get visits from cops.

MATCHLESS PAINT AND AUTO BODY. Complete with runs and drips.

CELLMATES CHILD CARE. Not with my kid, they don't.

These are, of course, extreme and fictitious cases. Most problems with company names are much more subtle and have to do with positioning. Your company's name should accurately reflect what you do.

When I first began my company, I named it Visual Communications Services, Inc. We were an ad agency, but we didn't sound like it. We got calls from people looking for duplicates of slides, for audiovisual equipment, and for multimedia shows for use at conventions.

Stubbornly, I stuck to the name for seventeen years. But when we moved our office in 1987 and had to reprint all our letterheads, envelopes, business cards, and forms, I gave in to the urging of my account executive, who said that it was too difficult to explain to prospects that we're really an ad agency and marketing communications firm. The consensus among the staff was to change the name to Gottry Advertising & Marketing, Inc.

Today, because the word *advertising* has fallen into almost the same category as *lawyer*, we've become The Gottry Communications Group, Inc. We can sell ourselves as the company that can handle any communications assignment: advertising, public relations, video, corporate events, newsletters, you name it.

The best approach is to give your business the "perfect" name right from the start and then stick with it. It's expensive to change a name (signs, forms, business cards, letterheads, and Yellow Pages ads all have to change). But the biggest disadvantage of a name change is that you lose the cumulative marketing benefits of name recognition, and you have to start over. This wasn't a big problem for us either time we changed our name because an ad agency has few clients and a limited number of prospects, and they can all grasp the change quickly.

On the other hand, if you've developed an insurmountable image problem (through no fault of your own) a name change could be your salvation. I'm still surprised that Tylenol didn't have to be reintroduced under a new brand name following the tampering incidents of a few years back.

Regardless of the name you ultimately choose, you'll have an easier time promoting your company if the name accurately describes the products or services you offer. If it's short and memorable, all the better.

How Are You Going to Position It?

Every company and every product needs what ad people call a "unique selling proposition," or USP. In short: What makes your company, product, or service different from every other competing company, product, or service? Why are you unique?

Your distinguishing benefit could be price, quality, variety, convenience, service, or a strong guarantee. Or maybe you just out-promote, out-advertise, and out-spend your competition.

Whatever it is, you must focus on your *competitive edge* and use it to build your business and your market share.

For Mercedes-Benz, that competitive edge is safety and quality German engineering.

For Maytag, it's dependability.

For Charmin bathroom tissue, it's "squeezable softness."

For Apple Computer, it's user-friendliness.

For United Airlines, it's "friendly skies."

I'm sure you can recall the slogans or unique selling propositions for scores, if not hundreds, of companies and brands. They have spent major amounts of money to make sure that you can.

Other companies, however, seem to have ongoing difficulty positioning themselves in the consumer's mind. They struggle with one ill-conceived idea after another. Certain fast-food chains and hotels come to mind. People simply don't know why these companies are different or better—or even *if* they are. The companies in question haven't determined who they are and, as a result, are unable to establish a strong selling proposition.

What makes The Gottry Communications Group unique? What is our USP? Simply stated, we hire topnotch creative people and place them in a company with (lately) low overhead and (lately) little fluff. So our clients get "big creative bang" for "little creative buck." In addition, we offer extensive experience and expertise in selected fields, such as aviation, home building, commercial real estate, publishing, and travel.

For the video division of our company, Corporate Channels, our unique selling proposition is that we can create quality videos at a fraction of the cost of our competitors because (1) most of the overhead for the video division (accounting, legal, phones, receptionist, rent, and so on) is absorbed by the advertising agency, (2) we have kept the cost of technology under control, and (3) we employ multitalented, highly skilled people who have an entrepreneurial spirit and are thus able to help build the company and have a share in the stakes.

One of the most effective ways to begin to focus on your unique selling proposition is to draft a concise *mission statement*. This statement should be relatively brief (it should fit on less than one page), and it should be widely circulated among your employees, your customers, your vendors, and your prospects. Your mission statement is, in effect, your reason for being in business. It helps you position your company.

There's nothing profound about my company's mission statement. It has two components: our mission, and how fulfilling that mission benefits us. The "benefits" section is important, because we want our employees to buy into the mission of the company, and most of them weren't around when it was drafted.

Your mission statement may focus on your desire to be known as the company that provides fast and dependable service, that does contract manufacturing to the strictest tolerances with the fewest rejected parts, or that offers the widest selection of a particular category of durable goods.

As we will discuss in subsequent chapters, your mission statement—and the way you choose to position your business—is only the starting point. It may only work for today. Times change, products change, and needs change. To remain a viable business in the years ahead, you will have to accept and adapt to change.

Our Mission

The mission of this company is to become PARTNERS IN SPIRIT AND PURPOSE with our clients, to enable them to more effectively sell their products or services to a larger market at a greater profit, while at the same time satisfying our need to be creative, fresh, and innovative, and, in the process, grow in our careers.

The Benefits to Us...

As we succeed in meeting this goal, we will—as a natural by-product—make a reasonable profit as a company. The result of this profit will be greater personal income for each of us, better short-term and long-range benefit programs, an enhanced working environment, and the acquisition of new tools to make us more productive in our jobs.

By performing our jobs to the best of our abilities, we will be able to demonstrate through our portfolios or résumés that we are highly skilled and knowledgeable members of our profession.

How Are You Going to Determine Your Investment Needs and Finance Them?

No matter how carefully a financial plan for a start-up business is drafted, no matter how detailed and thorough the planning, some costly things are going to be overlooked. I have yet to encounter any businessperson who didn't ultimately need much more money for the start-up than originally anticipated.

Conservatively, I would estimate that new businesses need 30 percent to 50 percent more capital than what they, in their wildest dreams, imagined they would need. And, in virtually every case, an insufficiently capitalized new business opens its doors with one side of the coffin lid nailed down.

To determine your investment needs, you'll need to take into account various hidden costs as well as inventory-control problems and outside costs. You also need to think about where your financing will come from, how you will handle cash flow, and how you will define your pro forma business equation.

Hidden Costs

It's vital that you explore, investigate, and understand all the hidden costs associated with an investment to maintain control over that investment.

A printing company I know of decided to build a new plant to accommodate its rapid growth. (This isn't a start-up situation, but the same sort of thing can happen with start-ups.) The printer ordered a huge multicolor printing press to go in the beautiful new building. Only when it arrived in crates did the printers discover that, when assembled, it would be too heavy for their brand-new concrete floor. At substantial cost, they had to break up the floor, haul it out in pieces, and pour a new, reinforced floor that offered three times the strength.

Another company, a start-up manufacturer of energy-efficient furnaces, ordered some robotic welding equipment and had to have its leased space rewired to handle the extra demand for electricity.

Yet another company purchased state-of-the-art computers that promised to make every employee more productive and efficient. The owner discovered that the machines themselves were only a small part of the investment. Each one required not only additional memory, but also higher-capacity hard drives, extensive backup systems, a variety of accelerator boards and video cards, and other goodies too numerous to mention. Of course, all the old software was outdated, so another major investment had to be made. And the lines of employees waiting for the output from the new laser printer could only be shortened through the purchase of additional laser printers. I know the details of this story firsthand. It happened at my company.

Inventory Control

Another common financial trap is inventory imbalance. The new business owner expects to sell a certain number of each of hundreds or thousands of items over a certain period of time. But then something unexpected happens. Half the products move off the shelves more quickly than projected, while the remainder just sit there. Realizing that he or she must now stock twice as many of the items that do sell in order to meet demand, the owner increases orders on those items. Now the business has a problem with display space, with warehousing, and with the fact that the business has money tied up in that portion of the inventory that simply isn't moving.

An inventory-based business must have product to sell and must be able to meet demand in a timely manner. Customers today are impatient; they want immediate gratification and will go where their needs can be met. By gathering as much information as possible on the sales trends in your industry—from trade journals, visits to the competition, and study of competing advertising—you will be able to do more accurate forecasting.

Outside Costs

You must also determine what outside resources and services your business will require, what they will cost, and whether they are readily available. The list could be endless: legal and accounting services, hazardous and nonhazardous waste disposal, recycling services, shipping and mail handling, advertising and direct mail, sign painting, phone system purchase and installation, architectural design services, construction, and so on. One-time costs will be included in your start-up budget; recurring costs will be a part of your operating budget. Thus, your initial capital must be sufficient to handle all of your start-up expenses, and your operating capital, sales, and cash flow must be able to meet or exceed your operating expenses.

Sources of Financing

Few businesses get established without some source of outside financing. And very few keep going without additional financing. As long as you remain in business, you will probably always be paying interest to someone for something you have financed.

Traditionally, business start-ups are financed through venture capitalists, family investors, second-mortgage loans, or equity financing through banks. One of your primary goals should be to find those sources of capital that do not require you to transfer control of your concepts, patents, or ownership to others. An investor can own your building without owning your business.

I have done everything within my power to avoid selling off pieces of my business under duress. I do not want to wake up some morning, go into my office, and find the new owner sitting in my chair. I want a new owner to take over when I'm ready for it, and when it is to my advantage.

Because I am protective about my equity position in my company, I do considerable financing through personal lines of credit at banks and through loans against the cash value of my life insurance policies. I have had many of my insurance policies for so long that I have accumulated considerable cash values. I also use receivables financing extensively. Those who choose this route must be aware of the fact that banks have limitations on how old those receivables can be. For lending purposes, my bank disallows *all* of the money due from a particular client if *any part* of that money is ninety days past due. Don't count on money the bank won't let you have.

Sales and Cash Flow

An essential part of the business forecasting process is to know what you will need in monthly sales and cash flow to operate the business and to determine whether it is feasible to attain that level of sales and cash flow. Some businesses simply can't be operated at a profit—or even at break-even levels—based on the way they are structured. An example would be a restaurant that doesn't have enough tables to serve the number of customers at a certain average meal cost that would be required to break even. Wishing it so won't make it happen. Neither will projecting a customer count based on beginning lunch service at 9:00 A.M. or continuing dinner service until 2:00 A.M. Traffic counts won't materialize during off hours. Most people eat lunch at lunchtime and dinner at dinnertime.

Your Pro Forma

Your company needs a pro forma business equation. That is, *how much must you sell at what price to how many customers over what time frame at what fixed cost in order to break even?* If you do not meet the pro forma, you will lose money. If you meet it exactly, you will break even. If you exceed it, you will make a profit.

If you are losing money, you must change at least one of the variables of the pro forma. You must increase your prices, increase your number of customers, reduce your fixed costs, or change your hours of operation.

If you invoice your customers expecting payment later, part of your pro forma must take into consideration what share of your customers will pay within terms (say, thirty days), what share will be late with payment (and how late), and how you will fund the interim. How much will the money you need to continue to operate cost you in terms of interest?

Any business—even one with a solid backlog of orders, good employees, and efficient production—can get into severe trouble or go under if cash flow is insufficient to sustain day-to-day operations. I know firsthand. That's always been one of my most nagging problems.

What Kind of Business Structure Are You Going to Establish?

Every business is viewed by the law as a "person" or "body." In other words, a legal entity with a legal name. The kind of person or legal entity the business is determines how it and its owners will be treated under the tax laws and other statutes.

In establishing your business, you will need to determine how you want to be treated by those laws, and you will have to become the compatible legal entity. The most common options are sole proprietorships, partnerships, and corporations.

Sole Proprietorship

In a sole proprietorship, you, the individual, are the company. Your equity in your business assets belongs to you, and your personal assets belong to the business. They cannot be separated. You are taxed as one entity, and the personal income tax rates apply to all of your income. Your personal tax return will include all the special forms that relate to the operation of your business, and you can usually charge all operating expenses and losses against your gross income.

This option has two major drawbacks. First, you have little or no legal insulation, such as you would have if your business were a corporation. If the business goes away, your house, car, and other possessions may go away, too, depending on how much debt you have accumulated. Second, if you plan to actively seek outside lenders, they may not perceive you as "distanced" enough from your business, and less likely to lend money for purposes they may not see as being of a purely business nature. They certainly won't want to lend you money to enhance your lifestyle. They want their loans secured and protected.

If your dream is to build a profitable, growing business, I would recommend looking at other options.

Partnership

A business partnership reminds me of a marriage. Two people, usually of widely diverse backgrounds but who think they will always understand each other and get along, come together under one roof. And then the trouble begins.

Unlike married couples, who can experience the bonds of sex and children and the benefits of marriage counseling, partners are held together by cellophane tape and bailing twine.

Of all the partnerships I have personally observed, not one has remained successful and intact over the long term. (I'm not including those partnerships that are, in essence, professional associations—medical practices, accounting firms, and the like. Their larger size and purpose for being, coupled with the individual accountability of the partners, give them a much greater success rate.) One partnership of two brothers failed miserably within two years, despite the fact that the business was growing and prospering. Being brothers, they let some minor details, such as written contracts, slip by them. The relationship was further complicated because one was the operating partner and the other was the not-so-silent silent partner.

If you think divorces can be ugly, you should be on hand when business partners split up. When a partnership dissolves, there are assets to divide. This usually precipitates war. Not too long ago, a front-page article in *The Wall Street Journal* told the story of the demise of Philip Johnson Architects, one of the most respected and well-known architectural firms in New York. The story described an "unresolvable conflict between Mr. Johnson and his longtime partner" and observed that "the profession is rife with stories of partners stiffing partners as firms shrink, restructure and dissolve."[2]

In my view, partnerships fail for three basic reasons. The first is that the partner who believes he or she is working the hardest has the perception that the other partner isn't pulling his or her share of the load.

The second is that if the partners have an equal voice in the operation of the business, a stalemate often develops on critical decisions, and the business becomes immobilized.

But the greatest cause of failure, from what I've witnessed, is that each partner can individually act on behalf of the partnership. Each partner can sign contracts, bring suits, and incur debt. Yet in each case, both partners are individually and jointly responsible for the decisions, legally bound by the actions of one of them, and liable for the debt. It is possible that just one ill-advised move can doom what both individuals initially believed would be a lasting and mutually beneficial relationship.

Basing a business on the hope that your partnership can beat the odds is like building a house on a sandy beach.

Incorporation

A corporation is a distinct and separate legal entity. It, in effect, has a life of its own. A corporation can go down without dragging its owners or shareholders along with it. In the event of failure, you are no more legally responsible for the debts of your corporation than you are for the debts of your next-door neighbor. I use the term *legally responsible* because I believe that, insofar as we are able, we are all *morally* responsible for the debt we incur, whether we incur it under the auspices of a corporation or not.

There are certain circumstances under which the courts may not uphold that protection. In these cases, the "corporate veil" is pierced. The attorneys for your creditors can argue that you did not adhere to corporate formalities, such as electing a board of directors or keeping minutes of shareholder and board meetings. The court could determine that your corporation was set up primarily for the purpose of isolating you from your obligations and responsibilities and thus could hold you personally liable.

If you have limited assets, have little experience in your field, and have not yet established a solid credit rating, your vendors or suppliers may seek an extraordinary measure of financial protection. If their confidence in your ability to succeed in business is low, they may insist that you personally guarantee the financial obligations of your corporation.

They may require that you—as a tenant in their office building, warehouse, or mall, as a borrower from their bank, or as a buyer of their raw materials, products, or services—pledge to pay them the money your corporation owes them in the event of corporate insolvency. For a very small business, personal guarantees have some meaning. For a larger small business, these guarantees mean next to nothing. Over the years, I have signed so many personal guarantees that if I were to sell all the assets of the business, plus everything I own personally, I'd still come up thousands of dollars short. For example, a personal guarantee on my five-year office lease at $4,000 per month calculates out to a debt of nearly a quarter of a million dollars. According to news reports, bank robbers average about $4,000 per stickup, so I'd be looking at knocking off sixty banks over five years just to pay the rent. (I'd also be looking at 240 to 560 years in the cooler for armed robbery.)

In tight economic times, sales mean everything to your suppliers, and they may waive their demand for a personal guarantee if you push them.

The real beauty of incorporation is that it provides the best legal and business context for future growth. As a corporation, you can attract outside investors, sell shares of the company, and, ultimately, go public with a stock offering—subject to all of the rules and regulations our government has devised to protect the innocent investor.

You will need to consult with your attorney about the laws of incorporation in your state to determine whether and when incorporation is the way for you to go. You can do it yourself in most states for from $50 to $100.

S Corporation

An S corporation—or closely held corporation—is a twist on the regular corporation that has been adopted by most states. Essentially, it involves a provision of federal tax law that permits the principal stockholder to pay the company's taxes and claim the company's losses on a separate tax return that is filed in conjunction with that individual's personal tax forms.

The advantages of the S corporation are that you don't pay taxes twice on the same income, and you are not double taxed when the time comes to sell assets or liquidate the company. This can be a very real benefit.

In determining the legal structure of your company, choose the option that puts you in the best position to obtain needed financing or investors, while providing the greatest measure of protection for your personal assets. Since, in general, lack of capital kills businesses, and availability of capital helps them grow and prosper, incorporation becomes the most attractive option.

How Many Employees Do You Need, and What Do They Have to Accomplish?

When it comes to personnel, the two great mistakes made by businesspeople are *understaffing* and *overstaffing*. The problems of each are obvious.

If you are understaffed, you are unable to meet the service, delivery, and deadline demands of your customers or clients. And if someone calls in sick or goes on vacation, your problems are compounded.

If you are overstaffed, you will often be paying people to sit around and do nothing. Customer service will be outstanding, however, because you may have two or three employees to handle the needs of every customer.

The problem for the small businessperson is to maintain the proper balance between the supply of employees and the demand of customers. The solution can be cross-training or the restructuring of specific jobs.

During the peak years of my business, I had eight people in the creative department who generated sufficient revenues to pay for themselves plus three people in the support areas. If I had needed to add a ninth creative person, the overhead associated with that person would have been apportioned among the eight income-producing staff members. The added burden would have been easy to bear.

The recession forced us to cut back to three income-producing people in the creative department, plus the three support persons. Due to our reduced work load, we now had fewer than half as many income-producing creative people carrying the load for the same number of support persons as we had before. Not only was the pro forma not working, but we would have to take on a higher percentage of new business (33 percent) to pay for one new person than the 12.5 percent we would have needed when we had eight people generating income.

We effectively dealt with this problem by computerizing some of the functions that were previously performed manually, by restructuring and eliminating some of the support positions, and by hiring an extremely efficient part-time person to take on the income-producing responsibilities that had been handled by an underworked full-time employee. This was the first of many steps we took (and are continuing to take) to make our company more productive and better able to meet the challenges that the recession and other changes in the business environment have forced upon us.

What Policies Will Apply to Those Employees?

There's a young pup (at least I think of twenty-five as young) who operates a small business in the same office building where I lease space. This likable, upbeat, young entrepreneur has been in business for three or four years and oversees a team of commissioned salespeople along with one salaried office assistant.

We've become friends, and he occasionally approaches me with questions about business. One day a few months ago he asked me: "My assistant will have been with me a year next week, and I was wondering, should I do something special? Should she get a vacation or a raise or something?"

My reply was, "What is your company policy? What does it say in your employee handbook?"

He looked at me with a totally blank expression on his face. "Handbook? What handbook? Do *you* have a handbook?"

I showed him a copy of our employee handbook. He was awestruck. I said, "Young Pup (not his real name), if you would like, I'll give you a copy of our handbook on computer disk. You can print it out, change the name of the company wherever it appears, make any other changes you want, and—presto—you'll have your very own employee handbook."

Most major corporations would never dream of operating today without setting forth all their employment practices and policies in writing. Yet many small-business owners feel they need not be concerned about such matters. Nothing could be further from the truth. Even if you have only one employee, even if your handbook has its beginning as a two- or three-page memo, begin today to put one together.

Without an employee handbook, you have no framework on which to base such matters as hiring and firing procedures, vacation and sick pay, raises and promotions, and a myriad of other matters. Included at the end of this chapter is an outline of some of the topics that are properly covered in an employee handbook.

I have some words of caution about compiling and distributing employee handbooks. First, you must make certain the policies apply fairly to all employees in a specific class. You can have some policies that apply to part-time employees, some that apply to full-time employees, and some for commissioned employees, but the policies for a specific group must apply to all persons in that group.

Second, remove any ambiguity from your policy statements. Clearly define your policies, and make certain they are easy to understand and apply.

Third, study the laws and labor practices that apply to your business. Make sure your handbook does not contain policies that contradict local, state, or federal law. Consult with an attorney for accuracy and compliance with applicable laws.

Fourth, most states interpret the contents of your employee handbook to be a part of an "employment contract." In other words, be careful what you promise in your handbook, and examine the various possible interpretations of each statement so that you don't get caught in a legal trap later. Again, have a competent attorney review the contents. You may discover that your attorney will advise against publishing an employee handbook, simply because of the fact that they are often interpreted as binding contracts in the courts. Many law firms do not have employee handbooks of their own for this very reason.

Finally, make sure that you follow through on the policies you've set forth. Prevent your day in court at the hands of a disgruntled employee who feels that you enforced your policies with some employees and not with others. The most critical case in which this could come up is in a suit alleging "wrongful discharge," wherein the former employee charges that you fired him or her without cause, or for violations of policies or procedures that were not applied or enforced equally and consistently among all employees.

Your First Plan

When you have developed your answers to these eight basic business questions and have written them down in logical sequence, you will have the essentials of your first business plan. I say "first" plan because no plan will ever be your final plan. As we will discuss later, your new business is likely to evolve and change over the years, and you will need to draft new plans, secure new financing, and perhaps change the very structure of your business. But with your first plan in place, it's time to move ahead!

I. Cover Page
Includes a statement about the hiring practices of the company—nondiscrimination, equal opportunity—and also clearly states that the "policies contained herein are subject to change without notice."

II. Mission Statement

III. Days and Hours of Operation
Includes policies regarding overtime and compensatory time off; "flextime" schedule policies, if offered; lunches and breaks.

IV. Vacation Policies
How vacation time is accrued, how vacations are scheduled, and how they are dealt with in the event of resignation or termination.

V. Sick Days
Includes policies regarding doctor and dentist appointments; sick day reimbursement (if offered by your company).

VI. Emergency Days
Which events qualify as emergencies, which ones do not.

VII. Paid Holidays
Covers special cases when holidays fall on weekends. (We offer varying religious holidays depending on the preference of the employee.)

VIII. Health Insurance
Summary of benefits; cost, if any, to employee.

**Figure 1. Sample Outline of the Basic Contents
of an Employee Handbook**

IX.   Life Insurance

X.   Disability Insurance

XI.   Medical Reimbursement Plan

XII.   Other Special Programs and Benefits
Retirement plans, profit-sharing plans, family care, etc.

XIII.   Policies Regarding Hiring, Firing, Promotion from Within

XIV.   Grievance Policy

XV.   Sexual Harassment Policy
Defines sexual harassment and includes remedies.

XVI.   Alcohol and Drug Testing Policies

XVII.   Miscellaneous Policies
Smoking, phone use, dress or uniforms, etc.

XVIII.   Pay Policies
Raises, bonuses, commissions.

XIX.   Job Descriptions
Specific job descriptions for each employee (one per book).

XX.   Acknowledgment
Employee signs and returns this form stating that he or she has received, read, and understands the policies contained in the book.

Figure 1. Sample Outline of the Basic Contents of an Employee Handbook (continued)

3

THE IMPLEMENTATION STAGE

There comes a day when the dreaming and planning stages have concluded, and it's time to actually start your business. As the result of the planning stage, you will have named your business, determined what products and services you will offer, chosen your location, established your pro forma, determined your staffing needs, and obtained your initial financing or investment capital.

Your next steps are all inextricably intertwined. I won't go into detail, since each business has its own specific requirements, and what may apply to a manufacturing operation will have little or no bearing on a retail or service business. But there are certain tasks that every new business-person must complete.

In the preopening, or setup, phase, you'll have to prepare your facility for business. The steps may include build-out of office space; remodeling of an existing facility; interior decorating; installation of phones, fixtures, computers, or manufacturing equipment; and purchasing of forms and supplies.

You will have to order raw materials or inventory and arrange for shipping, delivery, and warehousing, as well as for payment.

And you'll need to hire and train competent employees to get your business off to a positive start.

The primary goal is to make sure that all the right pieces of the puzzle come together at the same time and fit perfectly—or at least close enough to create the desired picture: a successful, well-run new venture.

Fill In the Missing Pieces

How many people do you know who are experts in every field—who know all there is to know about every subject? The answer, of course, is obvious. Yet for some reason, when we start a business, we are expected to know everything about every aspect of that business. It's simply not possible.

I have a friend who began an advertising agency about the same time I began mine. This man is a brilliant salesman. He knows how to network, prospect, gain an audience, and close the sale. As a result, his agency grew much more quickly than mine.

In some ways, I was envious. His accounts were major food companies, government agencies, and international conglomerates, while mine were small local companies. His staff was outgrowing his office space. I added people only when my staff was being stretched beyond reasonable expectations.

Yet, today, his agency—the one I envied—is long gone. He freely admits to me now that while he knew how to "schmooze" and sell, he didn't pay attention to the numbers. He didn't understand receivables, payables, cash flow, and long-term debt, and he didn't hire a competent manager who did.

The point of this illustration is: *Fill in the missing pieces.*

If you don't know finances, learn—or hire someone who already knows.

If you don't excel in sales, find someone who does.

If you aren't strong in customer service, look for someone who is.

The fewer missing pieces you fill in, the bigger your problems will become. And such problems seem to grow and multiply exponentially.

But what do you do when you're just starting out in business and you don't have the capital resources to hire all the right people for all the needed positions?

The answer is to seek information and help from both internal and external resources.

Internal Resources

When we employ a new person at The Gottry Communications Group, we make it very clear that we are not locking him or her into a specific job that will never change. The reason is that people have talents and skills, interests and possibilities that cannot be ascertained fully at the time of hiring. We want to enable people to grow in their careers, while making sure that all the tasks we've hired them to perform are being completed in a timely and efficient (read that: profitable) manner.

One of the things we've done to bring the best ideas forward is a variation on the old suggestion box. We call it the "Idea of the Month Club," or Innovations for Success.

The problem with suggestion boxes is that they provide little more than an opportunity to crab and complain with anonymity. There is no incentive to contribute meaningful ideas. Our Innovations for Success program provides two of the most time-honored incentives: *money* and *recognition*.

The original criteria for judging ideas were that they had to save the company a minimum of $50 per month or add a minimum of $50 to monthly income. (I realize that for many companies this is small potatoes, so you can make it $5,000 or $50,000, or whatever you want. The principle is the same.)

What we discovered through this program is that people have ideas—good ones. And if they're part of the team, they'll help us implement them.

There *are* drawbacks to such programs. People are always eager to redefine their jobs so that they can do exactly what they want to do—and do very little of what *you want* them to do, or *need* them to do, to operate a profitable business.

I had an employee who was hired to be an art director. It was his job to manipulate type and pictures or graphics into a pleasing, compelling, and often colorful design—an ad, brochure, mailer, poster, or whatever. To fulfill his tasks, he used a Macintosh computer loaded with various graphic design and illustration programs.

In the process of using these programs, he became both proficient in the use of computers and addicted to all of the newer, better, faster peripherals and software programs that can be added to them. He convinced me that he was the right guy in the right place at the right time to computerize all our job lists, purchase orders, time cards, and other records. Because I was eager to see all of this happen, I gave him the green light to proceed.

The result? While he was busy satisfying his computer addiction, his productivity, and that of those under his direction, slipped dramatically. I was no longer paying him for what I had hired him to do; I was paying him for what *he* wanted to do. The moral? Gain the ideas you want from your employees, but make sure you also gain the output you need from them.

Outside Sources of Help and Information

When it's not possible to employ the right person for every job, or when you can't obtain the information and ideas you need for success from your current pool of employees, you need to turn to outside sources for help.

Often, these resources are readily accessible and are not necessarily costly. Following are the ones I have found to be the most helpful, along with what they most effectively provide.

Books and Magazines: Sources of Information

You are reading *this* book because you believe it will provide you with at least one idea of enough value to compensate you for the purchase price. But this certainly isn't the only book on business that could benefit you. Read others. Many others. Read *The One-Minute Manager*, by Kenneth Blanchard and Spencer Johnson, and some books by Peter F. Drucker, if you haven't already read them.

Buy them, check them out of the public library, borrow them from friends. It doesn't necessarily cost money to learn. It costs time. True, time is money, but not *all* time is money. *Some* time is an investment. Time spent in sleep refreshes you for the next day. Time spent reading and learning gives you a foundation on which to build your business, your family, and your life.

If you find if difficult to set aside large or consecutive blocks of time for reading, magazines provide an excellent alternative. In fact, magazines, because of their frequency of publication, often provide a more up-to-date source of information than books. The latest in-depth news, information, and ideas are found in magazines.

My wife would tell you that I subscribe to more magazines than any living human being. I'm sure that's not true, but I do receive about sixty-five magazines each month (not counting numerous publications we receive on a complimentary basis simply because we are an ad agency). Some relate to my hobbies—boating, flying, and travel. A few provide information on computers and software. Others are specific to my industry or my clients' industries. But the most useful ones cover general business topics. They tell me what's happening locally, regionally, nationally, and globally. They provide clues to the changes, developments, and innovations that could help or hinder my business in the days ahead.

The three most important magazines to which I subscribe are: *Inc., Fortune,* and a local Twin Cities publication, *Corporate Report.* The first provides small-business information, the second tells me what the big boys and girls are doing and gives me a broader perspective, and the last supplies information on what is happening in my market— and provides some good business leads.

The minimum number of nonhobby, nonnews publications to which you subscribe should be *five.* In addition to *Inc., Fortune,* and your local business magazine, you should get the two leading publications in your industry. As you add to that list, include *Forbes, Business Week,* and every other publication related to your industry. If you have major clients in industries with which you are unfamiliar, add those related periodicals as well. (Do you see how easy it is to come up with sixty-five publications?)

Videos: A Resource for Training

Videos are certainly coming to the forefront as tools for training—and I'm not just saying this because my company has a subsidiary that produces videos.

Video has the ability to demonstrate in real time. That's something that books and magazines simply can't do.

In our company, we use readily available videos to train new employees on computer programs such as Microsoft Word, Quark XPress, Aldus Freehand, and Adobe Illustrator. We've discovered they offer a multitude of advantages:

1. Videos reduce the amount of time our staff has to spend in training new people. Because billable time is the key to our profits, time spent in training others is, in that respect, unproductive.

2. Videos can be used during off times, even after hours, when a trainer may not be available.

3. Videos are rewindable and repeatable. Your employees can go over steps and procedures they don't understand again and again, without feeling stupid or fearing that they are wasting the trainer's time. Such fear blocks learning, and the trainee often misses out on an important step.

4. A well-written, well-produced video is generally more thorough and detailed than personal training by individuals in the company. That's because videos are usually prepared by the company that, for example, designed the software program or the piece of equipment. I must quickly add that we've come across some wretched productions featuring so-called experts, so the buyer must be wary. The best companies will offer a money-back guarantee in the event you are not satisfied for any reason.

The effectiveness of video as a training tool can and should be tested at the completion of the training cycle. That is when your trainer can handle additional questions and evaluate performance. The trainer should have previewed the video so that she or he can explain any discrepancies between the content of the video and your standard operating procedures.

Software: A Source of Invaluable Assistance

I am continually amazed by what computers can do these days. When we installed our first office-wide computer system in 1982, it was little more than a collection of glorified typewriters. They could store written documents on floppy disks and could print out our mailing list on tractor-fed paper. We were forced to junk the entire system by 1987. The storage capacity, software, and overall capabilities did not meet the growing needs of our business, and the system could not be expanded to meet those needs.

Now we have local area networks, color scanners, laser printers, design programs, accounting software, and on and on it goes.

With the coming of age of computers, the level of assistance you can obtain from your desktop or laptop model is truly amazing. You can get low-cost helps (often built right into your word processing program) to check your spelling and verify your grammar. Even the smallest companies can obtain an accounting program for well under $100 that will write checks, balance the checkbook, handle general ledger and receivables aging functions, and prepare invoices and statements.

It's worth a trip to the computer software store every so often just to explore new options that may enable you to save time and money. You can also gain valuable information from one or more of the magazines published for your specific computer brand or platform.

Seminars: A Source for Advice

If you read the right local publications or have made it onto the right mailing lists, you'll learn about a variety of seminars and training programs. Some of these seminars, sadly, are run by hucksters who want to separate you from three or four or five hundred dollars. Thanks to the attention generated by sexual harassment cases, we've been "invited" to a number of seminars "of vital importance" on this topic. One of them cost $795 for one day. The mailer told us that this was a small price to pay when one considered the possibility of multimillion-dollar lawsuits.

Well, my company has had a written policy on sexual harassment for several years. Our policy is based on information we gleaned from a *free* seminar offered by a local law firm. We were invited even though we don't retain this particular group of lawyers.

Many accounting firms, law firms, and investment counselors offer free or low-cost seminars that can be of tremendous worth to you and your company. Take advantage of any that are of interest or potential value, as time permits.

Trade Associations: Sources of Support and Information

You can also obtain free or low-cost information from your trade association. They *want* your business to be successful. Many such associations have publications, information hotlines, and computer billboard/information-sharing services. If they're available, take advantage of them. They offer one of the best ways to learn from the experiences of others in your industry or profession.

Consultants: The Voices of Experience

I've heard that a *consultant* is defined as "any person who used to have a job." While it's true that there are many so-called experts who clearly are not, knowledgeable consultants are available in every field. They can provide you with the one thing you can't gain entirely on your own: They can give you the benefit of their *experience*. And they can share what they've learned through their contact with similar companies in similar situations.

Consulting is going to cost you something, though. So it's best to make your needs and expectations very clear and gain some assurance that the consultant you are considering can meet those needs and expectations.

A number of general sources for consultants are listed in the appendix to this book. Consultants who work within your specific field can often be located through your trade organization.

It's vital that you verify the credentials of every consultant you are considering so that you don't shell out your hard-earned money for people who can't deliver on their promises.

Peers: Sources of Support and Advice

Business is so competitive these days that it may be difficult to seek support and advice from peers within your specific field. However, it's quite easy to network with others on your management level through such groups as your chamber of commerce, or through service organizations, such as the Rotary Club.

Some of you may be thinking to yourselves, "Rotary? He has to be kidding! That's nothing but a bunch of old men who sit around and smoke cigars." I can't speak for every club everywhere, but I belong to a Rotary Club, and it's anything but that. It's made up of businesspeople, young and old, who are caring, giving, and involved. I lean on and learn from each of them. I could never afford to pay for some of the invaluable advice I've picked up both from the guest speakers at our meetings and from casual conversations with the other members.

In the process of expanding my circle of friendships among peers, I did discover one person in my industry who realizes that he and I do not have to be cutthroat competitors, because there is enough work for both of us. He happens to be the president and one of the owners of a larger advertising agency in the same office building where I lease space. He has been a source of good solid advice as well as of business leads—giving me names of companies he can't accept as clients because they compete with other clients of his firm. I, in return, try to do the same for him.

If you're open to it, you can form some interesting and unexpected alliances that can be of tremendous help to your business.

Your Own Team of Advisers: Sources of Hands-on Advice

Several people have a vested interest in your company and are among those who truly want you to succeed. They are your lawyer, your accountant, your insurance agent, your stockbroker, and your investors or stockholders. Your particular group may not include all of these, but they are people to whom you could, and should, turn for help.

Some companies formalize the advisory relationship with this group. Others rely on sporadic luncheons and phone calls to glean much helpful advice.

I prefer to follow the formal track (although in recent months I have neglected my carefully laid plans to meet with my group on a regular basis). My plan called for quarterly breakfast meetings with my attorney, my CPA, my insurance agent, and my brother, who is a minority stockholder and a vice president of the corporation. (You'll notice that I didn't include a stockbroker or investment counselor in the group. More on that later in this book.)

One significant word of caution. You are going to get differing opinions, advice, and even supporting evidence from different sources. Ultimately, it's your responsibility to sort out all the conflicting ideas to determine the most appropriate course of action.

As you develop the habit of searching for outside resources to help you fill in the missing pieces, you will discover that doing so is well worth your while, not only in the implementation stage, but in all subsequent stages of the business life cycle as well.

4

THE GROWTH STAGE

In the growth stage, and in just about every stage of business that follows, competition is a way of life. And competition can either immobilize or inspire you.

The essential thing to remember is that your business will not win all of the challenges it faces. You will not best your competition all of the time. In the advertising business, it is typical to compete against three or four other agencies for every piece of business. We consider ourselves very fortunate if we win the account 25 percent of the time.

As a businessperson you compete in several arenas. You compete for the best employees against companies that are larger and may be able to offer bigger salaries, more benefits, and greater opportunity for advancement.

As a buyer of outside services, you compete against other companies for the best products, terms, and delivery schedules from your vendors.

You compete for clients or customers. Generally, to compete successfully, you must offer the best product in the shortest time at the lowest price. That's not a small order to fill. It's called value.

Offering Customers Value

In a sound, growing economy, *value* is judged on the basis of *quality*. In times of recession and the following period of recovery, value is judged more on the basis of *price*—and often price alone. Partly because recent recessions seem to be deeper and more drawn out than those of the past, and partly because many of us are turning our backs on the excesses of the 1980s, we are conditioning ourselves to judge value primarily on the basis of price.

As Newton noted, "A body in motion tends to stay in motion until some outside force acts upon it." Applying this principle to the notion of value, it would take a protracted period of good economic times to reverse the trend—for quality to once again become the primary descriptor of value.

To offer value in today's economy, you must have the lowest price on the product or service that can effectively fulfill the needs of the customer. To achieve that end, you must control costs. That requires

- Tightly managed overhead
- The lowest cost or most efficient employees or outside labor force needed to produce a quality product
- The most up-to-date cost-saving technology available

Cost control takes on less significance only if you can offer the best or most innovative product on the market—one that has no equal at any price—or, if you are willing to operate on the lowest margin of profit, which may make you vulnerable to price wars.

The unfortunate truth about business in America is that there isn't enough room for everyone; the larger, well-capitalized companies want to grow and do not want the smaller, undercapitalized companies to stand in their way. The companies in the strongest financial position will always try to weed out those in the weakest position. That's how they gain market share. And that's what United Airlines and American Airlines are trying to do to other weaker carriers. They're cutting first-class fares by as much as 50 percent and coach fares by as much as 38 percent. If you ran an airline that had high debt, had limited assets, and was already losing money, how long do you think you could play this game?

Having What It Takes to Compete

If you want to grow, you have to play some aspect of the game smarter than the big guys who want to squash you. You need to control overhead, find eager employees, keep your business structure simple, make the best use of up-to-date technology, offer the best or most innovative product, and market your product or service effectively.

Control Overhead

Don't play the "glitz" game that your more flashy competitors may be playing. Stay away from the Class A high-rise office buildings with the marble lobbies and brass doorknobs. You really don't need them. Although image is important in many businesses, most of your clients don't want to get the feeling that they're paying for your expensive tastes. It's possible to achieve a substantial measure of the image you want or need without paying premium prices.

My business is situated in what is considered a Class B ten-story suburban office building. It's clean, well managed, and well maintained. The staff provides outstanding service, and the owners are willing to invest enough money in upgrades to keep the building looking sharp. The amenities—a convenience store, conference rooms, heated indoor parking, a travel agency, and a lunchroom—more than satisfy our needs.

Naturally, I would love to move into the premiere office building just three blocks away. That building offers bigger windows, spectacular views of a nature preserve and a lake, on-site child care, a shoeshine stand, a hair salon, lots of gleaming chrome and marble, and one of the finest award-winning restaurants in the Twin Cities.

But if I were to relocate to that building, my clients would swear that I was ripping them off. And I'd be paying nearly double the rent, which would make about as much business sense in a nonsense economy as a new Mercedes-Benz 600 SEL (which, of course, I'd certainly enjoy owning)!

Find Hungry, Eager Employees

As the old saying goes, "There's no substitute for experience." But, as much as I would like to employ experienced people, the nonsense economy has forced me to find a substitute. That substitute is the young person who is eager to work and prove himself or herself or the older employee who has perhaps gone through a career change and wants a new beginning.

Over the years, I have hired people with tremendous abilities and great drive who were being overlooked by other companies because they were too young, too old, or too something and didn't fit the same criteria as the rest of the employees.

When unemployment is high, you can find prospective employees with remarkable knowledge and skills.

Later in this book, we'll discuss in detail some ideas on how to gain the most from your employees. We'll talk about ways to reward producers, uncover the valuable ideas that your employees have, and build on them.

Keep Your Business Structure Simple

For decades, large corporations have been saddled with several layers of management that have cost them billions of dollars, yet have produced little or no meaningful, measurable return. To keep employees happy, top management has promoted them to positions for which they are not qualified and in which they perform little meaningful work. This phenomenon has not changed since Laurence J. Peter first described it in *The Peter Principle.* [3]

The up-and-down economy is changing how businesses are run and, in the process, what people do for an income. The jobs of those who are marginally productive have been eliminated, and advances in technology have had an impact on the kinds of jobs that are necessary and useful in our society.

Since the founding of this nation, we have evolved from an agricultural economy to an industrial economy to a service economy. Today, we are evolving into an information-based economy. Two hundred years ago, most people were farmers, plowing the fields behind a team of horses. Then came tractors, combines, milking machines, hybrid seeds, and better fertilizers and herbicides. Today, 2 percent of the population produces enough food for all of us—plus enough for much of the rest of the world. The plentiful farming jobs are long gone. The agricultural jobs that fueled our economy evolved into manufacturing jobs.

The Industrial Revolution created the machines that made farming more productive, that made manufacturing more efficient, and that allowed transportation to connect the peoples of the world. People immigrated to this country seeking opportunities in our steel mills, on our assembly lines, and at our construction sites where great skyscrapers were taking form.

Today, the most dramatic change of all is taking place. Twenty years ago, personal desktop computers didn't even exist in anyone's imagination—except perhaps in the minds of a few science fiction writers. What changes we've seen in that time! Computers are eliminating middle-management positions left and right. The number-crunching functions that once took days now take minutes, or even seconds.

Perhaps one of the reasons you started—or are considering starting—your own business is that your job was the victim of the three-horned demon of recession, the computer revolution, and corporate restructuring.

During the growth period of your business, you owe it to your employees, as well as to your bottom line, to resist the temptation to create jobs that aren't needed, that aren't productive, or that could be eliminated as the result of the slightest decline in sales or profits.

Do everything you can to protect your company from wasted levels of bureaucracy and middle management that extract profits while returning no measurable benefits. Keep your structure simple. Find ways to push yourself and your employees to the fullest potential.

Make the Best Use of Up-to-Date Technology

The right technologies, properly implemented, may give your company a competitive edge over larger, better-staffed companies. In the best-case scenario, that edge can be maintained, and you will build customer loyalty as a result. In the worst case scenario, your edge won't last, and the cost of keeping up with advances in technology will outstrip profits.

Our company "signed up" for the computer revolution well ahead of most other ad agencies. As a result, we were able to achieve some cost savings in design, typesetting, and printing that others couldn't offer. Our advantage was short-lived, though. They caught up. And, ultimately, it was the computer revolution in the area of graphic design that hurt us.

Anyone with a computer and a color monitor now thinks of herself or himself as a desktop graphic designer. Because value is now judged by price rather than quality, we hear prospective clients say, "I don't need you anymore. I have a computer and a secretary who can do what you do." Indeed, if the secretary has a sense of design, understands how to use the programs, can comprehend printing processes, and has a grasp of marketing principles and techniques, he or she can.

The fact is, however, that the great majority of today's new desktop advertising whizzes don't have a clue about what makes a well-designed ad, which is why there's so much garbage being passed off as advertising. One does not become a Rembrandt simply by possessing a canvas, a set of paints, and some brushes.

Our video production division faces similar challenges. As we tool up with the latest video recorders, cameras, and computerized special effects devices, we could be shot out of the saddle by some simple, affordable, high-definition digital technology that makes current videos look like they were photographed through nine layers of gauze.

Our experiences don't mean we'll turn our backs on technology. We still have to keep pace in a changing world. If we allow ourselves to drop too far behind, we may never be able to catch up.

Offer the Best or Most Innovative Product

You must offer a product that has no equal at any price or you must provide some meaningful, measurable, realistic benefit that your larger competitors can't—faster delivery or more personal service, for example.

In some way, you have to be different or better. Your point of difference doesn't necessarily have to be a major one. It can be something as simple as establishing a toll-free phone number for ordering, offering to take credit cards, or staying open later on weekends. It can mean making small product changes that make it easier to use, transport, or service your product. It can mean a longer warranty or a strong technical support department.

Simply look at what your most successful competitors are doing and go one better. Then, let your customers and prospects know what you are doing.

Market Your Product or Service Effectively

It matters little that you offer the most innovative product at the lowest price or provide service that has no equal, if your potential buyers don't know about you.

Selling

All of business is selling. If you can learn how to sell, or find people who can sell, you can succeed. Our agency (and video division) has somehow managed to survived innumerable ineffective salespeople. Over the years, we've had nearly a dozen gung-ho sales types convince us that they were the right people to make our company grow and prosper. Some of them were with us for nearly two years and never generated a single viable lead.

It wasn't until spring 1992, when out of near desperation I hired my wife as my account executive, that I discovered I could finally describe qualities I had been seeking in an effective, winning salesperson:

- Willingness—no, an *eagerness*—to make "cold calls"
- Persistent personality, yet one that is not abrasive
- Bright sense of humor and an outgoing nature
- Outstanding organizational skills
- Exacting follow-through
- Personal integrity—one whose word is as good as gold
- Genuine interest in the needs and wishes of the customer
- Perseverance—a person who is not discouraged by hearing the word *no* time and time again
- Someone who is not satisfied with his or her current income

Normally, I would not advise spouses to work together. In fact, in those rare instances where I have seen it work, I have marveled that anyone could spend both work hours and personal hours with the *same* person.

Yet, of all the hotshots who had ever walked in my door, Karla was the only one who possessed *all* of the qualities I just described. And because our responsibilities are both distinct and clearly defined, we never have the uncomfortable feeling that one of us is somehow becoming subservient to the other. In effect, we simply do our jobs and stay out of each other's way.

Your outside sales staff, on-site sales team, or telemarketing representatives are your keys to person-to-person or business-to-business direct sales. They are where it all begins...and ends. Regardness what other sales and marketing tools you use, they are the ones who actually close the sale or take the order.

Marketing Strategy Components

For most businesses, several other components can and should be considered when developing a marketing strategy. Basically, these components can be divided into seven general categories: media advertising, direct marketing, incentives and premiums, contests and promotions, point-of-purchase materials, public relations, and customer relations (or public contact).

1. Media Advertising

Media advertising includes radio and television, newspapers and magazines, outdoor and transit signage, and Yellow Pages placements.

The underlying purpose behind any media decision is to reach as much of your target audience as possible with as little waste as possible for the lowest cost possible. Obviously, you do not want to pay high rates to reach a huge audience that is unlikely to be interested in your product or service. Nor do you want to pay low rates simply because they are low if they reach nobody.

More than pure cost must be taken into account when determining how and where to advertise. You must consider the advantages and disadvantages of each medium and weigh them against your budget considerations.

Television

The cost of buying television time is directly related to the size of the audience viewing the spot at the time it airs. This can be measured in cost per thousand viewers, or in gross rating points (the cumulative size of the audience that will see your commercial). Audience size is *predicted* (not guaranteed) through the use of viewer surveys. Nielsen and Arbitron provide survey data to both television stations and advertising agencies that subscribe to their services.

Using this audience research information, you can determine how many men, women, teens, and children are likely to watch each specific show in each time period, and you can buy the appropriate time slots to reach your desired target audience.

You would, for example, be more likely to sell women's products on Phil Donahue's and Oprah Winfrey's talk shows or on the daytime soaps. You would have a better chance to sell beer, boats, and cars on NFL football telecasts. You would probably want to advertise Cocoa Puffs cereal, Barbie dolls, and Hot Wheels on Saturday morning kids' shows. The research, obviously, is used to make those decisions and support them.

Television offers a number of advantages not available with other media. For one thing, television is the only available medium that combines color, sound, music, motion, emotion, and demonstration. In addition, you have the possibility of speaking to a very broad audience while still being able to reach selected groups. If you need to target your audience even more directly than you can through specific programs, cable television channels offer an excellent alternative.

Of course, television does have its drawbacks. Television sales reps will tell you that they can get you on a local television station for less than the cost of radio, and, in many cases, this is true. But the fact remains that you will pay a rate for your spot based on audience size. For example, on one television station, you could pay as much as $6,000 for a 30-second spot during its top-rated prime-time program, or as little at $20 for the same spot between 1:00 A.M. and 6:00 A.M. While $20 may seem like a great rate, your spot running at 2:15 A.M. may reach only three to four hundred people. Of course, if you're selling a drug-free answer for insomniacs, that time slot may prove to be a good buy.

Companies sometimes run spots for the wrong reasons—ego, for example. It sounds good in a conversation to say you advertise on television. There is something glamorous about television, but is it your best investment? If you're not a trained actor, don't give in to the temptation to appear on camera (or even off-camera) yourself, unless you have a lot of public speaking experience. It's tougher to be an actor and develop a smooth delivery than it appears to be. It would be far better to include the cost of a professional in your budget.

Finally, a professionally-produced television commercial is usually going to cost significantly more than a radio spot or print ad. You can easily invest thousands of dollars to create the spot before it ever gets on the air. The average spot shown on network television costs $60,000 to produce; really elaborate ones cost $350,000 and up. And, if you want a celebrity to endorse your product, you could easily run the bill up into the millions.

Of course, there are some bargains out there. Some television stations will volunteer to produce your spot for you if you sign a contract to run it for an extended period of time; however, you may not be able to run that spot on other stations. More often than not, these spots are cheap looking and simply provide the viewing audience with more time to visit the bathroom. You can count on having to pay for the more elaborate elements that make a spot effective, including animation, original music, union talent, special effects, and endorsements by personalities.

Radio

Radio can be used effectively to reach select audiences. Differentiation by age is the easiest task to accomplish. As in the case of television, the makeup of the audience—age, sex, and so on—is ascertained by audience surveys and cost is determined by size of audience. In general, the highest rates for radio commercials are much lower than television. One reason is that it costs much less to properly equip, operate, and create programming for radio.

Radio is more readily and passively accessed than television. People listen to the radio in their cars, while doing dishes or cleaning the garage, or even at their desks at work. Television has to be actively engaged.

Radio offers the combined impact of sound, music, mood, and emotion. It doesn't offer motion, color, or demonstration, although an interesting demonstration effect can be conveyed through the use of sound effects. Radio can capture the imagination of the listener and create powerful images in the mind.

The cost of creating radio spots is substantially lower than television spots. An added bonus is that the advertiser can get a short turnaround time on radio. You can be on the air, in many cases, the same day you determine that you need to be.

Newspapers

Newspapers offer a number of distinct advantages over the broadcast media. For one, the reader can refer back to your message to note your phone number, address, and details of any special offer. Newspaper advertising is cost effective for purposes of testing special offers and incentives. Newspaper readers actively participate in the selection process; customers can tear a coupon out of the newspaper. It's not a background medium like radio.

Additionally, you can target your demographics based on the newspaper section in which you run your ad. That's why copier and computer ads run in the business section, hotel and restaurant offers run in travel or variety sections, and sports equipment ads run in the sports section.

Creative and production costs for a quality ad are much lower than the costs associated with television and radio, and newspapers offer quick turnarounds on deadlines. The lead time can be as short as two or three days, compared, for example, to forty-five days or more for most magazines.

There are a few downsides to consider with newspapers. Because newspaper readers include every segment of society, you can't target prospective customers as closely as with other media. A lot of competing messages often appear on the same page, and the quality of reproduction, except for preprinted color sections, is generally very poor. A newspaper is not the best place to show the beautiful sparkle of a diamond ring.

Newspapers have a short shelf life. They are generally disposed of in a day or two. When the next edition arrives, the previous one is forgotten.

Magazines

Magazines offer the capability to target extremely selective audiences. There are magazines for skiers, boaters, pilots, wrestling fans, Caribbean cruise lovers, golfers, quilters, "do-it-yourselfers," moviegoers, musicians, and on and on. No matter how obscure the subject, chances are there's a magazine (or two or three) published on that topic. Thousands of consumer and business magazines are published today. Most ad agencies and libraries subscribe to something called *Standard Rate & Data Service,* a set of books that lists all of the magazines and newspapers published today, along with their ad rates. *SRDS* also prints similar volumes for other media, including radio and television.

The quality of reproduction in magazines is generally far superior to that of newspapers, so you *can* show the sparkle in a diamond ring.

You can make special coupon offers, and, if your budget permits, you can create elaborate preprinted color inserts to bind into the magazine. (Perfume and cologne samples are examples of preprinted inserts.)

Generally, the shelf life of magazines is longer than that of newspapers—it can be a month or more. Some people save their magazines nearly forever.

Finally, the pass-along characteristics of magazines are excellent. Readership studies demonstrate that several people usually read a single copy of the typical magazine. This gives you more reach (a larger audience) for your investment.

Overlooked Advertising Forums

Consider buying advertising space on a transit system— bus, metro, railway—or buy the space sold in commuters' waiting areas and shelters. These channels are an excellent way to reach a large, untargeted audience without paying a premium for a specific billboard site in a certain geographic or demographic area.

The sales message must be extremely short, concise, and clear in any form of outdoor, transit, or bus stop advertising because the exposure time is very brief.

Yellow Pages Advertising

If you sell impulse items or need to generate a lot of walk-in traffic or phone inquiries, put together a great Yellow Pages ad. It's out there doing its job for a full year.

In fact, I would never consider operating a tire store, pizza delivery service, or limousine company without a great Yellow Pages ad.

One pitfall of this kind of advertising is the tendency of certain industries to try to outdo each other in terms of the size of their ads and the use of color. The result is a lot of full-page ads screaming to attract attention at a cost that can become outlandish. Yellow Pages ads are not cheap.

Should You Hire an Agency?

There are three reasons why companies work with advertising agencies:

1. A good creative team knows how to how to create a sales message that cuts through the clutter to help their clients achieve a competitive edge that will capture, hold, and convince the intended audience.

2. Companies can gain the experience and advice of a solid team with a variety of skills, so they don't have to use their own full-time people and add to their overhead. They pay only for the services they need and use.

3. Because an ad agency is *not* a part of the day-to-day operation of the company, it can bring a fresh perspective to the problem or situation.

There is no magic formula for determining your advertising budget. It's not set by calculating some percentage of sales or gross profit or net profit. Neither is it determined by spending part of what's left. The only way to determine budget is to decide what you want to accomplish and then determine what you need to do to achieve that objective.

Always bear in mind that *the purpose of advertising is to sell.* Obviously, you can't spend more money to sell your product or service than you would raise in income in the process, so the definition has to be expanded: *The purpose of advertising is to sell more of your product or service to a larger market at a greater profit.*

If you choose to work with an advertising agency, public relations firm, or outside marketing counselor, here are some hints to follow to make the relationship more productive:

- *Listen to your consultants.* They *want* your advertising to work. Their success is directly related to yours.

- *View these people as partners, not adversaries.* Give them the information they need to do the job. They will respect your need for confidentiality when it comes to industry-sensitive information, but you'll get better advice and more effective advertising if you don't keep them in the dark.

- *Respect the fresh point of view these people have to offer.* An ad agency won't necessarily do things the way you would do them. But these specialists are going to look at things from the perspective of your potential customers and design the message to speak to them.

- *Don't discourage them from bringing a wide range of ideas to you.* Sometimes the idea that seems a little too far out is the one that will work. But if you continually ridicule unusual agency ideas, you'll see nothing more than typical, even flat ideas. Remember one of the things you're paying these people for is their creativity.

Figure 2. How to Get the Most From an Ad Agency

- Don't beat the agency down on price. A good relationship has to be a win-win situation. An agency that is giving away their work won't be around to do more of it, and you will lose everything you've invested to get them up to speed on your company and your products.

- If you have asked for an estimate on a job, you are partially responsible for making sure that estimate is not exceeded. Don't make minor or unnecessary subjective changes. Don't cut costs on a great idea, because that is likely to reduce its effectiveness.

- Don't quit too soon. You will make mistakes. Your agency will make mistakes. So take a look at the overall relationship and ask these questions before you drop the agency:

  1. Given an adjustment based on the state of the economy, are we better off or worse off as a result of working with this agency?

  2. Are we keeping pace with the competition in terms of sales, product development, creativity of the message, and cost effectiveness of our advertising?

  3. Are we doing everything we can to help the agency do its job?

  4. If we are being approached by another agency, do we have solid reasons to believe they could do a better job?

  5. Are we getting the attention and service we need?

**Figure 2. How to Get the Most From an Ad Agency
(continued)**

Advertising should not cost—it should pay. If you are spending money on advertising without seeing a corresponding increase in sales, there is either something wrong with your advertising or something wrong with your product, whether it's price, quality, utility, or even the location of your business. If you cannot discern the underlying reasons, turn to specialists outside your company for help.

2. Direct Marketing: Making the Connection

Direct marketing includes direct mail, catalog sales, home shopping programs on cable television, and telemarketing—those annoying phone calls that always occur just when you're sitting down to dinner.

Direct mail can be an extremely effective way to target your message to specific geographic or demographic markets. Your selection of mailing lists can be made by using a wide range of criteria, including ZIP code, specific industries or professions, likely purchasers (based on past purchasing habits), and so on.

A direct-mail package doesn't necessarily have to be a two-dimensional envelope containing a letter, a brochure, an order card, and a reply envelope. It can be strikingly creative, even three-dimensional, for added impact.

You wouldn't believe some of the strange things we've mailed on behalf of our clients—4,000 slices of real toast in imprinted boxes, 1,000 regulation tennis balls attached to miniature tennis courts, 20,000 packages of wildflower seeds in specially printed seed packets (and this wasn't for a seed company), 5,000 balsa wood glider airplanes, 1,000 cassettes of newly recorded piano music, 75,000 printed pieces that contained a dozen little "windows" to pull open (each with a message behind it), 500 imprinted miniature basketballs, and 5,000 packages of Gummy Bears. Each mailing went to a select market, and each generated an outstanding response.

The key to every successful direct-mail program is to select the right lists. Direct-mail list brokers specialize in assembling lists covering a wide range of categories. You can direct your message to doctors, dentists, lawyers, teachers, physicists, computer owners, fertilizer manufacturers, farmers—you name it. In most cases, brokers will sell you a portion of the list to test before you commit to the entire list.

When developing a direct-mail plan, make certain that the pro forma works. Given the cost of creating, producing, and sending the mailing, can you sell an adequate quantity of your product at a price that will cover expenses and still make a profit?

The most profitable, ongoing direct-mail strategies are clubs and continuity programs, which secure repeat or ongoing orders from customers.

Clubs

Book, record, and video clubs generally make a wonderful initial offer ("Choose any 5 for $1") and rely on members to order a minimum number of products over a given time period at slightly higher than street prices.

Continuity Programs

The purpose of continuity programs is to get the customer to purchase the first item in a set, with the promise that they can "cancel at any time." Continuity offers can cover anything from leather-bound classic books or video libraries to model cars or porcelain dolls.

Catalogs

A number of successful businesses have been built through the use of catalog marketing. You're familiar with many of them: L.L. Bean, Land's End, The Sharper Image, Sporty's Pilot Shop, and Spiegel, among others.

New specialized catalogs are cropping up continually. If you offer a specialized product line, you may want to add catalog marketing to your menu of sales tactics.

Telemarketing

The two forms of telemarketing are outbound and inbound. Outbound calls are unsolicited calls placed to selected prospects by the marketer—or what I call "dinner calls." If you are inclined to want to market using this technique, please observe the following:

1. Train your callers to sound like real people, instead of robots reading scripts. Have people you know call them to spot check how they sound.

2. Tell them to be courteous, and allow the person called to interrupt and end the call.

3. Prepare them to be severely abused by some of the people they call.

I hate to admit that something that I personally find to be so obnoxious and invading can be an effective sales method, but it is. And I'm actually nice to those callers who respect my time and my privacy, and sound like thinking human beings.

Inbound telemarketing relies on an outbound advertising message to be successful. The marketer operates a direct-mail program or runs print or broadcast ads that tell prospective buyers, "Operators are standing by, call toll-free at 1-800, etc." Most consumers respond more favorably to this approach.

3. Incentives and Premiums

This category encompasses special sales, events, discount coupons, "early bird" specials, bonus programs, free promotional items sent to prospective customers, and specialty advertising.

You can gear your incentives toward your sales staff (the more they sell, the more perks they get) or toward customers ("Buy one, get one free," "Fifty cents off your next purchase," "Free gift enclosed").

Incentives and premiums should be an important part of your marketing program if you are introducing a new consumer product—especially if the product requires a change in consumer brand loyalty.

4. Contests and Promotions

Contests and promotions can be used to attract prospects and customers to your product or service or to encourage your salespeople to perform beyond normal expectations.

Whereas incentives and premiums tend to involve a sale to the customer, contests and promotions are traffic builders, generally not tied directly to a purchase. The goal may be to elicit the sale, but a purchase is not mandatory. In fact, there are strict laws that prevent this direct connection.

Promotions can be as varied as the imaginations of the businesspeople who create them. For decades, both small communities and large shopping malls have relied on visits from Santa Claus to draw children and their parents to the stores. Retailers use sidewalk sales, white sales, midnight sales, and every other kind of sale to generate excitement. And companies that sell business-to-business often hold open houses and new product expos, or offer free seminars to their customers and prospects.

In addition to building traffic, contests and promotions are effective in acquiring names to add to a prospect file or direct-mail list.

5. Point-of-Purchase Materials

Point-of-purchase materials can range from an elaborate, animated floor display supplied by a manufacturer or supplier to a simple hand-painted window sign or interior banner that calls attention to the special of the week.

Your storefront, signs, and window displays or posters are all part of point-of-purchase selling. In service businesses, the lobby plays that role. That's why green marble, mahogany reception desks, and overstuffed leather chairs are so popular with law firms, ad agencies, and investment/financial planning companies.

In the typical retail environment, point-of-purchase is a mixture of floor displays, counter displays, shelf-talkers, suspended banners, videotaped sales messages, end cap displays, and live product demonstrations. Because these items are all competing for the customer's attention, often in a cluttered environment, the creation of effective point-of-purchase materials has become both art and science, practiced by experts in copywriting and design.

A key point to remember is that if everything stands out, nothing stands out. In a crowded theater, no one thinks it's strange if everyone laughs at the same time, but if one person laughs while everyone else is quiet, that person stands out. Every designer of point-of-purchase materials wants his or her design to be "the one person who laughs when all others are silent."

6. *Public Relations*

Public relations (PR) encompasses all of the activities involved in the dissemination of information about the company and its people, products, and services. These activities include issuing news releases, holding press conferences, and staging events that are covered by the press. PR is considered by many to be "free advertising" because the company does not pay for advertising space or commercial time to get the message out to the public. However, effective PR is not free, because a qualified practitioner must prepare news releases and search out contacts in the media. That person may be either a paid staff member or an outside consultant or public relations firm. In either case, it costs something.

Public relations efforts pay off well when the news is both positive and newsworthy. When the company is prospering, when the stock is climbing, when the new products are wonderful, when the humanitarian needs of the public are being met, you can almost count on good press. But if you're simply operating an honest company, making a good, dependable product, and providing good service, you're not making news.

With an advertising campaign, you have substantial control. You can determine *when* your message will appear, *where* it will appear, exactly *what* it will say, and *what size* (or what length) it will be. You have control over *how often* it is repeated. With a public relations campaign, you lose that control. You don't know in advance whether your message will appear, when it will appear, where it will appear, how often it will run, or even whether it will have a positive tone when it does appear.

What you do gain from an effective public relations campaign is perceived credibility. People trust news reports, articles, and reviews more than they trust paid advertising.

7. Customer Relations (Public Contact)

The most powerful, memorable, and effective advertising campaign in the world can't counter the effects of rude, inconsiderate employees.

The entire matter of customer relations can be distilled into a set of simple rules that should be nailed to the rest room walls, taped to the cash register, printed on every telephone, and sewn inside every employee's clothing:

> Smile, be clean, smell good, dress appropriately, give the customers your undivided attention, move quickly, be considerate of their time, respect their opinions, don't argue with them, and don't hang up the phone until after the customer does.

If you and all of your employees follow these guidelines, your company will never be justly criticized for poor customer relations, and you will have the power of positive public contact working on your behalf.

The Hazards of Growth

You can derive a great deal of excitement and personal gratification from watching your company grow. But I have seen many companies go under as the result of too rapid growth—growth for which they were not adequately prepared.

The first problem they encounter is that cash flow lags behind, so current obligations can't be met and payments on long-term debt cannot be made.

The second problem is that companies experiencing rapid growth cannot service their customers at a satisfactory level, and their reputation is tarnished.

The third problem is that they have increased their costs by adding staff, space, inventory, or machinery to meet the surge in demand. When the inevitable downturn occurs, they find themselves saddled with high overhead.

While it's exciting to take risks to grow—and every small businessperson has to do so—there is one risk that I believe is not worth taking. That's putting all your eggs in one basket.

That huge new account—that grand customer that accounts for 70 to 90 percent of sales—looks good at first. But when it goes away, as they all do eventually, your company could easily become history.

We recently signed on a client that was a vendor for one of the largest high-tech companies in the Twin Cities, a corporate giant that, at its peak, employed 35,000 people. A combination of recession, questionable management decisions, and dramatic changes in the industry struck down this Goliath, and its work force has tumbled to less than 7,000. As a result, our client's largest customer is no longer placing orders with the vendor.

We worked together to develop a strategy to obtain new business from a wider range of smaller customers, and, fortunately, it worked quickly enough to save our client's business. The company now has as many orders as it can handle, and the business won't be threatened if one or two of those smaller customers goes away.

The corollary to the "all-in-one" customer is the all-in-one vendor.

One local company was built on a foundation of being the exclusive distributor for a certain product line. Those products accounted for over 85 percent of the company's sales. When the manufacturer pulled the sales and distribution contract and awarded it to a competitor—well, you can guess what happened.

The obvious point I'm making is to be patient about growth. Take small, deliberate steps toward your goals. Work tirelessly to increase your customer base. And have a plan that does not leave you vulnerable as the result of increased overhead, inadequate cash flow, or the loss of a major client or supplier.

Strategies for Growth

If you are impatient about growth—or in the financial position to grow quickly—you can draw on a variety of strategies.

The first, and perhaps most obvious, is *merger*. In its ideal form, two or more companies with the same structure, sales, and assets join in a deal that is easily executed because of their similarity. This situation is nearly perfect, because it does not require any form of cash or stock transaction, since both (or all) parties are bringing the same value to the table. But when one company has more net worth or higher annual sales or profits than the other(s), the deal becomes more complicated.

In a merger, the companies are united into a new company that may or may not have a new name. From a marketing standpoint, it is advisable to retain the name of the company with the strongest image and market presence, to take advantage of the cumulative effect of all of the advertising, signage or visibility, and customer loyalty that were in place before the merger.

The second strategy for growth is *acquisition*. In this case, one individual or company purchases the assets, customer base, and goodwill of another company. The owner of the acquired company more than likely will have no day-to-day involvement in the acquiring company and will receive cash or stock as the result of the transaction.

The worst-case scenario is that the former owner receives no cash but simply has his or her debt assumed by the new owner. In any case, the former owner is essentially "cashing out" of the business he or she built, and the new owner is counting on the continued loyalty of the company's customer base.

The company that emerges as the result of acquisition will usually retain the name of the acquiring company, although occasionally the names of the companies are blended.

For the business owner who is considering either retirement or new and different business pursuits, making the business available to companies interested in growth by acquisition can be an attractive option.

The third strategy for growth is to add *new locations*. This approach is particularly effective in growing a retail business. If you are successful and profitable in one geographic area or one shopping mall, for example, adding new locations in new areas or in additional malls can be the key to growth.

The city where I live and work is the home of the Mall of America, the largest indoor shopping, recreation, and entertainment complex in the United States. It's so large that a theme park, Knott's Camp Snoopy, occupies the central atrium. It's also so large that ten retailers—including four or five well-known nationwide chain-store operations—each have opened two stores in different areas of the mall. These retailers recognized that most shoppers won't be able to visit the entire mall in a single day, so two stores are needed to take advantage of the location.

Recognizing the fact that downtown St. Paul businesses won't retain a downtown Minneapolis accounting firm, and vice versa, the accountants I use achieved significant growth by opening additional locations, including one in each downtown area.

Can you imagine the Walton family still being among the wealthiest in America if Sam Walton's vision had been limited to opening only one Wal-Mart? If you have a good business idea, and it's generating a healthy profit, carefully weigh the advantages that opening additional locations may offer. But don't continue to pour unreasonable amounts of money into unprofitable locations hoping they'll turn around. That kind of wishful thinking has taken down many a company that could have survived on a single location.

The fourth strategy for growth is to *franchise* your business. This tactic presumes that the idea is, indeed, franchisable. The advantage of franchising your business concept is that you do not have to assume the financial risks associated with opening new locations. Furthermore, if the plan is successful, you can achieve a long-term, steady cash flow.

The fifth strategy for growth is to offer *expanded products or services.* The most obvious things are often overlooked, such as adding service to a sales operation, or sales to a service-based company. I have been told that, in most automobile dealerships, the profits generated by the service department exceed those of both new and used car sales combined. If that's true in the automobile business, it could be a factor in your field as well.

In the mid-1970s, we discovered that we were paying an outside service (and charging our clients) thousands of dollars annually for the relatively simple task of shooting photostats (black-and-white enlargements and reductions of artwork). We saw this as an opportunity to generate more profit for ourselves and simply bought a stat camera and converted a small storage room into a darkroom. The investment was small, the return was significant, and the improved turnaround meant that we could service our clients better.

There are, I'm sure, opportunities to expand your services and increase your profits right in front of you, waiting to be discovered. Look for them. And don't send cash to outside services if you can keep that cash in your company.

The sixth strategy for growth is to fully *develop both horizontal and vertical markets.* If you sell computers and you discover that your computers are ideally suited to, say, medical clinics, you should work to develop that vertical market and target your sales and marketing efforts to that field. If you sell computers that, by virtue of price, are well suited to a broad spectrum of business, develop that horizontal market. Don't just sell computers. Sell them to specific markets. Discover who needs them, who wants them, and who will buy them.

I once heard the story of a woman who manufactured greeting cards that contained lots of interesting "sparkles"—sequins, gemstones, and the like. She discovered that what her customers wanted weren't her cards but all the glitter she put on them. She now does a booming business selling bags of this stuff to handicraft types.

The seventh strategy for growth—one that may serve as the foundation for all of the others—is to *find sources of new capital.* Bring in new investors so that you can move ahead with the other elements of your plan for growth.

One of the sources of new capital can be an ESOP—an employee stock ownership plan. Through a leveraged ESOP, your employees are able to buy a part of your company using someone else's money. With this plan, the ESOP borrows money from an outside lender to buy stock in the company. The company makes pretax contributions to the ESOP over the long term, and the ESOP uses those contributions to repay the loan.

An ESOP is, in effect, a profit-sharing plan with special nuances. Normally, the participants in a 401(K) plan can't buy and hold the employer's stock. But an ESOP can. And the result of such "vested interest" in the company is usually heightened employee morale and increased performance.

Some owners may seek new money for the purpose of covering up or rectifying past management mistakes. Investors are quick to spot this ploy, and if they are willing to invest at all, it will be because they see a bright future for the company in spite of the problems and will often invest with the stipulation that they take control of the company.

My friend, Young Pup, had quite a desire for rapid growth, so he spent all his time putting together a plan for potential investors when he should have been out selling. As a result, he found himself in a fairly large financial jam. This situation made investors shy away, and anyone still interested in investing wanted control. Young Pup decided it would be in his best interest to grow more slowly and deliberately. That is the course he has charted for his company, and it appears to be working. He is finding his way out of debt through a combination of hard work, sound pricing strategy, and excellent customer service.

Growth for the sake of growth is not a sound idea. There has to be a valid business basis for growth. As the result of "diversification mania" that was running rampant in the 1980s, large corporations found themselves with unprofitable divisions in areas in which they had no prior experience. In the 1990s, these same corporations are selling off the divisions that are not related to the primary focus of their businesses.

No matter how carefully planned or diverse your strategy for growth may be, no matter how solid your marketing plan, no matter how experienced your sales team, remember this one crucial statement: To be a successful, growing company, you must offer a meaningful product, supported by timely delivery, backed by competent service, and sold at a competitive price. If you do, you will be able to build on your reputation. If you don't, word of mouth will kill you—recession or not.

5

THE PRESERVATION AND EVOLUTION STAGES

W hen things are going well—business is moving along —the tendency is to pull back, become more conservative, and protect what one already has.

Perhaps inventory can be cut a bit. Perhaps that new piece of equipment can wait. No need to hire someone to fill a specific need. It can wait. Why not save some money, and cut back on advertising and marketing?

Preservation Versus Change

If your only goal is to continue business as usual, you'll discover that your employees will become stagnant, uninspired, and lackluster. Your business will be like a swamp—nothing fresh will ever flow into it, and the stale water will never flow out.

Just "holding on" isn't going to make it any easier to earn a profit. Now is the time to take some calculated risks, to embrace new ideas about how to perform the old tasks, to explore new technologies—to put FANAFI ("Find a Need and Fill It") to work.

Businesses that want to survive will change because people's needs change. To apply the FANAFI principle, you have to ask—and answer—some tough questions. Is your business still in tune with your customers' valid needs, and are you filling them? Are you willing to move ahead to the next inevitable stage in the business life cycle? Is your business ready, willing, and able to evolve?

Willingness to Evolve

If you are not prepared to accept the fact that your business must change with the passage of time, you shouldn't be in business. Imagine owning a "yuppie" health club but refusing to install aerobicycles, stair climbers, rowing machines, or Nautilus or Cybex equipment. It would be just you, your free weights, your punching bag, and eight or ten paying customers. Or imagine operating a music store that sold only 8-track tapes and long-playing record albums. You'd have lo-fi, and low sales.

The key to ongoing success in business is the willingness to evolve—to be alert to changes in needs, interests, and tastes, and to change with them.

At my company we have found a number of ways to maintain our awareness of change. We watch the news. We read trade journals. We pay particularly close attention to technological advances. And for years, we have had something called the *focus committee.*

The focus committee came into existence because I realized that it was impossible for me to keep on top of all of the changes in our industry and in technology that affected our industry. Originally, I relied on the same two employees as participants on the committee. After noting that these people offered the same point of view in every meeting, I opened up the process to every employee of the company. The ideas I hear each month are pure dynamite!

How does it work? Before a meeting, each "member of the month" is given two pages of general topics to ponder. Space is provided under each item to make notes. Some of the topics we regularly cover include

- Industry trends that could or will affect us
- Technological developments that could or will affect us
- Investments we need to make to maintain leadership
- Departmental operation review
- Projection of departmental needs and changes
- Departmental troubleshooting/problem solving
- Account prospects/recommendations/areas of interest
- Time use and efficiency/scheduling issues
- Evaluation of our creative product
- Critique of our service levels
- Personal career goals and aspirations

Through our focus meetings, we've developed new services to offer, we've explored new markets, we've found ways to improve cash flow, and we've determined how to meet our computer and software needs on a tight budget.

The focus meetings also provide an opportunity for review and analysis of the changing technologies that could diminish our competitive advantage.

Some Reasons for Caution

Evolution may require major changes in the way you do business—in what products and services you offer and how, and at what price, you deliver them. It may require significant investments in equipment that could be worthless in an unreasonably short time—in technology that could quickly become outmoded.

A word of caution is in order here. Some business owners try to force their businesses to become something they aren't—and shouldn't be. They try to redefine their niche—for reasons of ego or whatever—and end up trying to "fix something that ain't broke."

Here's an example. A Twin Cities company began operation several years ago in a rundown (but not unsafe) warehouse building, selling furniture and mattresses at a discount. Throughout the years, the company invested a fortune in creating an image of being discounters—selling low because of low overhead. And the market believed the image. The company sold great volumes and opened more "warehouse" locations.

But somewhere along the line someone in the upper levels of management decided that sales could be increased if the company built fancy self-standing buildings (not attached to a shopping mall or any other businesses). This suddenly made them "destination" stores. Customers had to plan ahead and go out of their way to shop there. Naturally, prices had to be increased to pay for the added overhead.

I was not too surprised when I recently visited one of their locations and discovered that the "sale" prices were higher than those of a well-reputed major department store, that the parking lot was empty, and that it was easy to get the attention of a salesperson, since I was one of only two customers in the store. Now, I don't have access to this company's private financial information, and it may be doing just fine, but it doesn't appear that way, and it could be that the redefinition of themselves and their market has hurt them.

The point is this: if you are operating a business that is successfully filling a need at a profit, don't tamper with the formula for no real reason. It could backfire on you.

This said, I still can't overemphasize that the key to continued success throughout the life of every business is simply FANAFI—Find a Need and Fill It. If needs change, the products and services that businesses must provide to fulfill them must change as well. You are likely to find that the business of your dreams, the business you operate the day you open it, and your business of tomorrow are three distinctly different things. Don't fight market-driven evolution. And don't evolve unless that evolution is market driven. In short, use change to your advantage.

6

THE SELLING/DIVESTING STAGE

There will come a day when you've had enough. You'll be older. You'll be tired. You'll have grown weary of competition, and you'll want out.

It will be time to sell the company, to let someone else take over the reigns, or to cease operations altogether. As you march toward that day, it is vital that you are psychologically prepared for the accompanying trauma. Leaving your lifelong business without an alternate plan that fulfills your mental, social, and even spiritual needs could be devastating.

My accountant/friend Dudley Ryan tells the story of a retired entrepreneur who sold his business a number of years ago yet who still goes every day to a small, inexpensive office he rented in a downtown building. He spends his days planning, scheming, and dreaming, and helping younger businesspeople plan, scheme, and dream. He's retired and he has no real income, but he's making a difference, because he hasn't put his mind out to pasture.

It is also crucial that you make adequate preparations from a tax standpoint, as the sale of a business can have a variety of tax consequences. It would be impossible to delineate them all here, because they vary from state to state and from year to year. To avoid unpleasant surprises, obtain sound advice from your accountant and your lawyer before you are faced with the realities of this stage of the business life cycle.

Seven Ways to Leave Your Business

There are seven basic ways to bring your involvement with your business to a conclusion. The first is simply to *close the doors*—to sell off your assets and pocket the money minus taxes, of course. This may become your only option if you are among those optimistic souls who believe that their lives will go on forever. If you hold this belief, you may be tempted to hold on to your business too long and sell too late. Liquidation may become your only choice.

There are some advantages to this approach. You don't have to worry about what's going to happen to your business after you're gone. And there won't be any fighting over who gains control—or how. But the disadvantages, in most cases, clearly outweigh the advantages. You won't realize the equity of all the sweat you've put into your business—the value of your name and reputation, for example. The cash you receive won't be based on true market value. You'll simply get a few dollars for the current market value of your buildings, fixtures, inventory, and equipment. And you'll be watching your dream dissolve right in front of your eyes.

The second way to conclude your business is through *bankruptcy*—an unpleasant alternative discussed in some greater detail in Chapter 7.

The third way is to *sell it outright*—perhaps through a banker, lawyer, accountant, or business broker. In this case, you have little real say in determining who takes over your good name and won't know how honest, competent, or well intentioned the new owners are. But at least by following this path, you should be able to benefit financially from the goodwill you've created over the years.

The fourth option is to *sell your business to your partners* (if a partnership) *or to your key employees.* This option offers a way to place your business in the hands of people you know, value, and trust. It's also a great way to repay years of dedicated service and should provide your faithful employees with more job security than they would have if you simply sold your business to strangers.

The ideal approach would be to hand-pick one person for the leadership role and let that person bring the other employees into the fold. An outside party should handle the negotiations, to minimize the employer-employee or buyer-seller conflicts.

In the case of a partnership, you should preplan for this possibility. At the inception of your business, you should have drafted a "Buy/Sell" agreement so that the transfer of your equity can be orderly and take place without misunderstanding or dispute.

The fifth approach is to *bring your company public.* This option assumes that your company is profitable, growing, and in an industry with a bright future. Depending on how the public offering is structured, you can maintain control by owning the majority of the stock, or you can put your control at risk by selling the majority of the stock to investors. As long as your company remains profitable, your shareholders and board of directors should realize the value of supporting your role as the CEO/president, even if you no longer maintain your position as majority shareholder. At the first signs of distress, however, you could be gone. You would still have the equity in the stock you do own, of course.

According to Richard Young of Bayfields, Inc., who has helped a great number of companies go public, if you want to take this step, you must be willing to undergo a considerable amount of scrutiny. Every aspect of your business will be investigated, probed, and explored. You must have a substantiated record of three to five years of growth in earnings. Young also cautions that you must be prepared to wait to fully "cash out." Underwriters are not likely to sell the founder's stock until the third to fifth round of financing has been completed and proven replacement management is in place.

The sixth strategy is to *turn your company over to your children* or other heirs. One of the most common problems with this tactic is that your children, love them as you do, may be incompetent and unable to effectively run the business. The other problem is that your longtime employees may resent the fact that there's nothing in this plan for them, and they may not willingly or eagerly pledge their allegiance to your beloved offspring.

If you have planned the course your business will take—and if that plan involves your children—you may want to begin the process early. You can slowly "gift" your business to your children at the current rate of $10,000 per year per child ($20,000 per year if your spouse is part of the plan). In aggregate, you can gift up to $600,000 of your estate tax free, and your heirs can realize the benefits of the appreciation of those assets without additional federal tax liabilities. If you wait until your will kicks in, your heirs will be subject to the taxes on the market value at that time, less the (current) $600,000 exemption. It's a way to beat inflation, but watch your newspapers and talk to your accountant. These numbers—and the rules—could change with the next session of Congress.

The seventh plan is the *employee stock ownership plan,* or *ESOP*. ESOPs provide a method of turning the ownership of your company over to your employees on a bit-by-bit basis. If you respect and appreciate your employees, an ESOP is an excellent exit vehicle. You must make sure that you have a willing and capable leader to replace you, and your company's long-term debt level must be relatively low and under control. You can generally assume that it will take five to ten years until you receive your last check.

You may also be able to combine these plans for making your exit. For example, you can combine a public offering with an ESOP, or an ESOP with gifting to your children.

Have a Plan

No matter which path you choose to follow, the divestiture of your company will necessarily involve some planning. You will need the help of your accountant to plan a suitable tax strategy, and you will need the assistance of both your accountant and an outside business counselor to determine the fair market value of your company, its goodwill, and its assets.

Early in the process, you will also want to get your attorney involved. Whatever plan you choose, a thick stack of complex legal documents will be part of the picture.

If you handle the transition well, you should be able to enjoy the rewards of your hard work in the years to come.

7

THE ALTERNATE ROUTE: DOWNSIZING, BANKRUPTCY, AND STARTING OVER

When I began writing this book, my businesses, both the advertising agency and the video production company, were racing along. Even throughout our 1991 fiscal year, which ended on February 29, 1992, we showed steady profits. The recession was both deep and widespread at that time, yet we weren't really feeling its impact.

Every week, I saw (and still see) a computer printout of the hours my creative group billed during the previous week. Every week, I received positive news. We weren't making huge profits, but our weekly income exceeded our weekly expenses.

Every month, I prepared (and still prepare) a more detailed profit and loss statement. I use a simplified form I had designed, rather than the standard accepted accounting version, because I get to the real bottom line much more quickly.

On the "assets" side I naturally include cash in checking and savings, marketable securities, sound receivables, and work in process. On the liabilities side I deduct payables to suppliers, bank loans, taxes, my next payroll, and other short-term debt. All through 1991 and early 1992, the assets always exceeded the liabilities, with the spread growing every month.

In fact, sales activity and billings in March 1992, the first month of our new fiscal year, were very high, and the reports continued to look good. With confidence in our ongoing success, and a firm belief that our nation's economy was entering recovery, I left the blustery winter weather of Minneapolis for the warmth and sunshine of Palm Springs, California, to begin writing what I was *sure* would be a totally positive, encouraging, uplifting business book (though probably not as honest, heartfelt, and real as it has become as the result of my more recent business challenges).

On my return from California, one of the first things I did was take a close look at our job list—the weekly record of new and continuing assignments. I noticed that this list was rather slim. But considering how busy we had been over the past year or two, we welcomed this as an opportunity to take a short "breather." After all, I reasoned, people cannot operate at peak efficiency under tremendous deadline pressure forever.

As the days and weeks passed, however, this "short breather" had begun to turn into a long dry spell. As I reviewed the weekly time reports, it was clear that we were generating less revenue than it cost to operate the business. New sales were slow to come in, and the job list continued to shrink.

To make matters worse, one of our major clients had eliminated its Minneapolis office, consolidated its operations in Chicago, and shifted the person with whom we had worked to another area of responsibility. Our new contact person believed that advertising and marketing were unnecessary expenses, and nearly 10 percent of our business was lost to that belief.

More bad news followed. Another client—part of a huge conglomerate—was told by corporate headquarters to cut $400,000 from its already approved budget immediately. We were $330,000 of that cut.

Yet another client had a product banned by the Food and Drug Administration—the product for which we did advertising. With no product, there would be no ads.

I was nothing short of devastated. But with over two decades invested in my business, and little interest in doing anything else, I realized I had to take the necessary steps to save the company. In the back of my mind, though, I knew it wouldn't be easy.

Downsizing: Our Strategy

Over the course of the next few weeks, I discovered there were seven crucial steps to my business recovery—steps I am still taking today.

Acknowledge the Problem

When things have been going well for a long time, most business owners typically assume that they will continue to go well. They ignore any evidence to the contrary. They don't want to acknowledge that anything is wrong and that something has to be done to fix it. Maybe it's ego. None of us likes to admit to failure, whether we caused it ourselves or it was thrust upon us.

To make the changes necessary to stay in business, I had to face the unpleasant fact that I had a very real problem and that the problem was big enough to destroy the business. Only then could I draw from my resources and make the tough decisions I knew had to be made.

Cut Quickly and Deeply

I'm basically a really nice guy. All my friends tell me so. My accountant confirms it every time we talk. Naturally, we talked a lot during this difficult period. I told him that I was struggling with the reality that I would probably be forced to lay off part of my staff.

After taking a closer look at my situation, he said, "You're just too nice, Steve. You have to realize that it's either *some* of you now, or *all* of you later." I hated hearing those words, but I knew he was right.

The most dreadful responsibility the owner of any business ever faces is having to lay off good, loyal employees.

I can only imagine how Robert Stempel, former chairman of General Motors, felt when he announced the closing of twenty-five plants and the layoff of 74,000 people.[4] I hope his heart bled. I hope he agonized for each and every one of them. I hope big business isn't as cold as we've often been led to believe.

In my case, I had to lay off only two employees. But, judging from the way I felt, it might as well have been 75,000.

One was a man whose wife was due to give birth just three months later. He had recently sold his house and bought another one, but that deal had failed to close at the last minute because of an unfortunate legal technicality. For all practical purposes, he and his expecting wife were homeless. Yet I had no choice.

The other was a woman who was getting married five weeks after the date of her layoff. Both she and her fiancé were young and just getting a start in their chosen careers.

I hurt for both of them. My heart ached. I wanted to say, "Don't worry, we'll make it work somehow. We'll find a way for you to stay with the company."

But in business, one does what has to be done.

I made numerous other cuts. I slashed travel and entertainment expenses, dropped my club memberships, eliminated 25 percent of my leased office space, canceled my indoor heated garage space (a real sacrifice in Minnesota, where the temperatures can drop to minus 30 degrees in the winter), and made dozens of other adjustments in the way I spent money.

"Hope," they say, "springs eternal." And hope delayed these and many more tough decisions beyond when they should have been made. I had to make additional cuts—severe cuts—more than a year later. Without taking this action, though, I would not have been in any position to rebuild my business. I would have simply been another bankruptcy statistic.

Renegotiate Debt

As the result of my "economic downturn," my payments to my creditors were delayed well beyond terms. Many of them became nervous. *I* became nervous. Then I asked myself, "Do any of my creditors, being of sound mind, want to force me to go under? What would they get then? Wouldn't I—and they—be much better off if we worked together to renegotiate the debt?"

The loss of certain clients meant that we would no longer be needing the services of certain vendors. Specifically, we wouldn't be advertising in certain publications that were targeted to industries in which we no longer worked. These were the first vendors with whom we renegotiated our outstanding debt. This was fairly simple and straightforward. We promised to send them *something*, no matter how small an amount, every week or every month until the debt was paid. They agreed to the plan. Because we have established credibility with them as a result, and because we are successfully rebuilding the business, we believe we can count on them to work with us if we reenter the lost industry segments—although our new working relationship may depend on different arrangements.

Other vendors—the ones with whom we needed to maintain an ongoing relationship in order to meet our clients' needs—provided a different challenge. They wanted to make sure we weren't adding new debt faster than we were paying off old invoices. Fortunately, our drastic reductions in overhead have enabled us to get ahead of the curve.

Then we looked at long-term debt—equipment payments and the like. We calculated that by selling one asset, we could eliminate three debts and consolidate two others, cutting our overhead by another $1,400 per month. That's not a lot of money to most businesses, but in the midst of our struggle for survival, it seemed like $14 million.

Finally, we reviewed our office lease and decided that since we were within eighteen months of renewal, we could approach our landlord to negotiate a rate that reflected the recent declines in the commercial real estate market. The landlord cooperated.

Do Away With the Toys

The Mercedes and the Fiat convertible were among the first things out the door. Then the airplane and hangar went up for sale, along with some of the older computers that were sitting around idle.

As we walked from office to office, we discovered that much of what we owned fell into the "toy" category. These things didn't do anything for our growth or profitability. Did we really *need* an air hockey table or video games to create effective advertising?

We were careful not to sell things that still had reasonable utility, or that we would need to repurchase later. We also fought the temptation to "fire sale" some of the items just to get some fast cash.

But the toys had to go, and go they did.

Get Good Advice

Going it alone in times of economic hardship and business restructuring is not a good idea. No matter where you stand, you cannot get a clear view of the entire problem, nor can you see all of the possible solutions. I relied heavily on my support system (a concept I will discuss in detail in Chapter 8).

My best advice during this period came from a man who had been through a major downsizing in the past and from the head of another ad agency that had experienced recent problems similar to mine. If you are ever faced with the pain of downsizing, it will surprise you to discover how many sources of helpful advice will become available to you if you are open to them.

Focus on Areas of Proven Expertise and Success

My ad agency friend's advice during this period was to focus on areas in which we have knowledge and experience. In seeking new clients to replace the lost ones, we focused on fields where we felt we had particular expertise: book marketing, real estate, home building and home improvements, computers and software, medical research, tourism and hospitality, and college marketing. We went after, and are still pursuing, clients in those fields. And it's working.

Draft a Plan for Recovery

We were faced with precious little time to think about and draft an elaborate, detailed plan for recovery. But we realized that a plan, no matter how simple, was a crucial key to our future as a company.

Our plan incorporated the following straightforward points:

- Our number one job will be *sales.* Everyone on the team will be expected to keep alert for possibilities, prospect individually, and participate in proposals and presentations. Sales will be viewed as a cooperative team effort. The goal in all cases will be to actively and aggressively ask for and seek the sale. Sales activity will be carefully tracked.

- Our number two job will be to *cut expenses* everywhere we can. We will attempt to streamline our support staff to the point where one highly competent full-time person can handle phones, media, computer input, general ledgers, invoice preparation, bill paying, mailing list management, proofreading, assistance in traffic, filing, and general sales support services.

- We will set up, once and for all, any systems that could or should be handled on computer. When operational, these systems will not be tinkered with, nor will any programs be changed, except by virtue of upgrades that do not require major adjustments to operating procedures. We cannot afford to invest time rethinking systems and procedures at the expense of sales and billings for creative time.

- We will handle immediate overload situations by developing a strong network of freelancers for both video and advertising/graphic design.

- We will invoice as quickly as possible on completion of jobs, so that cash will be available to meet urgent demands.

- We will suspend all computer and software purchases except for those upgrades to our current programs that are genuinely useful and for needed storage disks and cartridges, until such time as profits allow them and real needs demand them.

- We will evaluate our sales, cash, and receivables position on a weekly basis and make necessary cuts and adjustments as rapidly as possible.

- As we rebuild, we will not hire any creative persons who do not have a solid book of printed samples, who do not have computer design experience, or who need extensive training to get up to speed. We can't afford to be a training ground for new people on new technologies, although with the constant changes in technology, some staff retraining will always be inevitable.

- Over the long term, we will employ new people with an upgraded level of creative competence; we will try to find people who are better at this business than we are.

- We will be quicker to terminate those employees who do not measure up to our standards or the standards of our clients. There will be no "free rides" for anyone.

- Those who say "It can't be done" will have to get out of the way of those who are doing it—or are willing to do it!

- We will explore every way possible to keep more of our billed dollars in-house while sending fewer dollars to outside vendors—by hiring people with multiple skills to prepare layouts, do illustrations, shoot photographs, and so on.

- We will reduce current debt over the long term, and we will do everything possible to avoid taking on new debt.

- We will not add new programs, benefits, equipment, or people until we can readily afford to do so.

- We will still do what we can to provide for the futures of key employees, through benefits, including a retirement program that is available to all employees. It's costly, but it helps build loyalty.

- We will sell hard, work smart, and practice patience, understanding, and tolerance. We will always keep our senses of humor alive.

- We will balance the demands of work with the needs of our families and our personal needs for various escapes from the pressures of our jobs.

These steps are simple and straightforward, yet so easily overlooked. As I've tried to illustrate throughout this book, often it's not the big blunders that put companies under; it's the little day-to-day slip-ups and oversights that lead to disaster. Downsizing can be the first crucial step toward correcting the slip-ups. But without acknowledging the problem, reacting quickly, making deep cuts, getting good advice, and drafting a sound new plan, the slip-ups will end the life of a beloved company. You will come face to face with the most dreaded of all of the stages in the business life cycle.

Bankruptcy

The curtain could have—maybe should have—been lowered on my fledgling business in the fall of 1971. At the time, I had a small two-room office in a dilapidated old building in south Minneapolis. My rent was a whopping

$120 per month. I had one employee in addition to myself. And I had two clients.

One of them was World Wide Pictures, the motion picture division of Billy Graham's organization. These people were wonderful; they liked my work, paid their bills on time, and were positive and uplifting, with tremendous integrity.

The other was a company based in Detroit. These people were an absolute nightmare. They were demanding, paid slowly, and haggled on price. Eventually they went away, but not before they stuck me for $22,000.

That, friends, was a real problem for a dinky little two-person operation that was started with $125 in the bank and had no investors behind it. I took a quick look at my payables and discovered that I owed two printers nearly $14,000. I didn't have that kind of money, and I didn't know where I could ever get it.

I had two choices. I could let my dream slip away and declare bankruptcy. Or I could call the printers, tell them what had happened, and arrange a payment plan. I chose the latter.

To my surprise, the owners of both companies said that they would be happy to work with me and that I should simply send them whatever I could afford every month. One of them refused to do any additional work for me; the other said he'd gladly continue to work with me as long as I didn't get deeper in debt.

Every month for nearly three years I sent a payment to each of them. I delivered my final payment—in person— to the one who had agreed to continue to work with me, LeRoy Undis of Custom Craftsman Printing. He commemorated the occasion by taking me to dinner at a wonderful steak house, followed by great seats at an exciting NHL hockey game.

Two decades later, my company continues to buy printing from Custom Craftsman. And when I need help with a charitable printing project, I know where to turn. Had I declared bankruptcy in 1971, I would not have had the satisfaction of personally delivering that hard-earned final payment on my debt. And I would not have had a valued friend in LeRoy Undis for all these years.

In 1992-93, I woke up from a comfortable "sleep" with a similar nightmare. When I sorted the bills I owed in one pile and my receivables in another, the news simply was not good. Most of my advisers and interested onlookers said, "C'mon, Steve. Bite the bullet and shut this thing down. Your debt outruns your receivables by a ratio of three to one. Save yourself the headaches, worries, and sleepless nights and declare bankruptcy. You can always start over."

They were right. I *could* start over. I could wipe the slate clean. I could stick it to the suppliers I'd had relationships with for several years. For what? To save myself the "sleepless nights"? Thank you, but I'll sleep better knowing I did everything possible to pay off my debts.

One of my largest outstanding debts was with my landlord. And he was justifiably getting impatient. Following the downsizing of my office (which I did twice, actually), I began to sell off my excess furniture and equipment. I would immediately write a check for the amount of each sale and hand carry the checks to the building owner's management office. The landlord couldn't believe it. He said, "Most people would just vacate the building and leave us hanging." Well, readers, I honestly like to think that I'm not "most people."

The point I'm trying to make should be clear. If you and I, as businesspeople, have even the slightest hope of living up to our commitments and meeting our obligations, we should do everything within our power to fulfill them. Bankruptcy shouldn't be viewed as an easy out.

I recognize that there are circumstances under which bankruptcy is clearly unavoidable. There comes a time in the life of some businesses when there simply is no other alternative. The debt load is staggering, and the prospects for new sales, followed by sufficient profits, are bleak. There are few assets to liquidate for cash.

It's important, in such cases, to know when to call it quits. One must lock the door before incurring even more debt and hurting even more creditors, and minimize personal exposure as much as possible.

If you have kept a close watch on your finances—sales, expenses, receivables—you will know when "Hurricane Andrew" is brewing and where its track will take it. Try to anticipate bankruptcy and plan for it at least three months in advance. This will give you an opportunity to retain and work with a competent attorney, in conjunction with your accountant, to chart the proper course of action.

Your accountant will be able to present a clear picture of your current situation, including the details of your assets and liabilities, as well as an overview of the tax implications of any moves you are contemplating.

Your attorney will use that information to make a recommendation as to whether you should file Chapter 11 or Chapter 7 bankruptcy. Chapter 11 provides for a court-ordered plan for reorganization and payment of your creditors while offering you enough protection to operate your business while rebuilding. Chapter 7 is the statement, "I am closing the doors, and the spoils will be divided among all those who have a legitimate claim against the business, based on how those claims are secured."

Generally, the government has first claim for any back taxes owed, followed by payroll due to employees, then by secured creditors, then by unsecured creditors, who may receive ten cents or less on the dollar.

About the only hope you have is that your attorney may be able to devise a plan under which you are one of the employees to whom payroll may be due, or under which you may be a secured creditor. Again, I want to emphasize that the purpose of such a plan should not be to cheat your creditors out of any money that is due them.

If you have gone through or will soon submit yourself to bankruptcy, you must immediately move ahead to the next phase of your business career. Do not dwell on it. Do not think of yourself as a failure. You will have another opportunity for success. Colonel Harlan Sanders was well into his sixties when he came up with the notion of Kentucky Fried Chicken. It's never too late to make another start in business!

The Second Start-up

I have asked myself the following questions hundreds, possibly even thousands, of times: "What happens if my business goes under? What will I do then? Will I go to work for someone else?"

The answer, at least from my perspective today is, "I will regroup, begin again, and start a new business." I will not work for someone else—at least not for very long. I am an entrepreneur. I want to do my own thing, captain my own company, chart my own destiny.

Any businessperson who is fueled by desire and fired by determination will never settle for anything less than trying again. There will be no doubts or hesitations—a new business will be born.

If you or I are ever faced with the need to start over, we will have learned enough from our triumphs, mistakes, omissions, and miscalculations to do a better job of it the second time around.

What Is a Second Start-up?

The most common definition of *second start-up* is a new business begun after an entrepreneur's first business fails. He or she then dreams a new dream, drafts a new plan, and starts over.

But from another perspective, a second start-up can take place when an owner sells a successful business and reinvests the proceeds to begin another one. No business failure is involved.

A third view is that a second start-up can be the opening of a new location, the formation of a subsidiary division, or the establishment of a business unrelated to, yet operated concurrently with, the first. I have some experience in this area, as the result of the start-up of our video division, some seventeen years after we first opened the advertising agency. Getting it up and running was, in many respects, more difficult than getting the ad agency established. Had we not been able to take advantage of the agency's phones, office space, sales and support staff, and related talents, the video subsidiary would have been shut down within twelve to eighteen months. It simply didn't generate the level of sales activity necessary to support it in the beginning.

But the perspective from which I can share the most relevant insights is that of a businessperson who has watched his successful business crumble and has done everything possible to rebuild it through what has essentially amounted to a unique form of second start-up.

Our Story

I shared previously how we had lost most of our clients over a very brief time. This situation brought both a shock to the ego and tremendous economic strain. Our capital reserves were depleted, and we were losing thousands of dollars every week, month after month.

But what I haven't mentioned was that most of my employees decided to bail out of what they saw as a rapidly sinking ship. Many of them had been with me for three, five, or eight years or more, but they decided that although the captain may choose to go down with the ship, they had no desire to join him. Two of them left to form their own competing agency in the basement of one of the partner's homes. Two left for other jobs. One left for unemployment. And one stuck with me. She had to. She is my wife. As she says so frequently, "It's in my job description."

My entire team today is fresh, aggressive, and new. And what a group they are! We all have T-shirts proclaiming: "Official Member: *The Dream Team:* The Gottry Communications Group."

The Dream Team is going through a second start-up together. We are a new business. We have lost our old clients, said "so long" to our former employees, and kissed all of the toys and luxuries of the past good-bye. But, believe it or not, we're having fun.

We have a lot of hard work and difficult times ahead of us. The pay increases will be few and far between. The bonuses will be on hold for a while longer. Each member of the team is aware of the risks, and is willing to put in extra hours to make the company succeed.

Our Plan

What are we doing to increase our odds of survival? Part of the plan was laid out earlier in this chapter, in the section on downsizing.

The rest of the plan will sound familiar, since the principles have already been touched on:

1. We're going to do things differently. We're going to adhere as closely as we can to the simple guidelines we've set forth. We're going to be sticklers for the details that spell a difference in the real world of business and turn our backs on the meaningless drivel that doesn't produce anything for the bottom line.

2. We're going to learn from our mistakes. We're going to work smart, service our clients better, compete more effectively on price, and sell ourselves when times are good and we're busy, instead of waiting until the bottom falls out before we spring into action. We're going to watch our receivables more closely and collect them more quickly.

3. We're going to take different risks. We're going to go after higher-quality clients, and get more "edgy" in our approach to the advertising we create for our clients.

4. We're going to invest our profits wisely. We're going to resist temptation—no expensive toys, flashy cars, or five-star hotels. If it doesn't add to our bottom line, we don't need it.

5. We're going to fill in the pieces that were missing last time. We'll start by listening to the advice of people we trust.

6. We're going to make important decisions more quickly—especially those related to hiring and firing. We won't put up with dead wood in our lean, mean organization.

7. We're going to be a *team*. There will be no room for jealousy, bickering, or hotshot loners. If we're successful, it will be because we all had a hand in it.

If this plan doesn't work, we won't be around to talk about it. But I believe that common sense in business *does* work, even in a nonsense economy. I plan to be one of those who proves it!

PART TWO

Building on Your Assets

8

YOURSELF

Y ou, as an entrepreneur, are the greatest single asset your company has. It was your drive and your dream that created your company, probably out of little or nothing if your company is like so many other self-made ventures.

What are the unique attributes that you bring to your company, and how can you make the most of them to build a better future for you and your employees?

Your Enthusiasm

No one can be a "Rah-Rah!" cheerleader all the time. But enthusiasm, or the lack of it, is catching. As the owner of your business, your attitude sets the tone for the entire company.

It can be more than a little difficult to remain positive and upbeat if the economy is attacking your bottom line. Yet during the past two decades as a small businessperson, I've been through enough setbacks to realize that they are only temporary.

One of the wonderful things about being the boss is that I can fix things that are wrong. When I correct a particular problem, I find that my enthusiasm for my business is rekindled, my hope restored.

I take advantage of my enthusiasm by bringing the team together in a staff meeting, praising everyone for a job well done, and pointing out all the positive things that are happening in our business. That spirit is invariably caught by each of them, and they go through the week with an intensity and energy that exceeds my expectations.

Enthusiasm is like a dose of multivitamins. It's needed daily. Without that dose, your company will become sluggish and lackluster.

Your Attitudes

I believe that people can have only one of two attitudes: positive or negative. We have the opportunity, independent of our circumstances, to deliberately choose which of those attitudes will govern our daily lives.

It's easy to make that choice, to say "I will not dwell on the negative. I will believe what I've heard from Norman Vincent Peale and all those other advocates of positive thinking, and I will live a life of positive attitudes."

It's far more difficult to *live* that choice—to practice what we preach, and actually approach each day with a positive outlook.

One of the first things you see every morning plants negative thoughts in your mind: your daily newspaper. The headlines blast you with news of war, crime, natural disasters, drug busts, the homeless, unemployment, business failures, strikes, layoffs, environmental pollution, the deficit, and another loss by your favorite team.

And now you're expected to go to work with a smile on your face?

Well, you do your best. But then an employee who has a key business proposal due today calls in sick. The mail brings no checks—only bills. And the client you thought you had in the bag phones to tell you that your competitor made a better offer. You have a five-minute yogurt lunch at your desk because things are piling up on you. A brief power failure in the afternoon causes the office's computers to lose everything that wasn't just backed up.

At the end of the day, you skip the long lines waiting for the aerobicycle at your health club in favor of the long lines of traffic on the freeway. You arrive home to the news that your ninth-grader got a D in Spanish and an F in physical education. (How could *anyone* flunk PE?)

How do you maintain a positive attitude after a day like that?

By viewing the great tapestry of your life from a distance, rather than focusing on the small threads that are out of place, on the slight frays around the edges, or on that little rip that doesn't really have an impact on the beauty of the work.

You can gain that perspective by following a few simple strategies.

The first is to visualize yourself, your business, and the day just ahead of you as successes. Start each day recalling three positive things that happened the previous day. Note in your mind or on paper three positive goals you know you can meet today. It doesn't matter how big they are, how small they are, or whether you accomplish anything else in your day. As long as you meet your three goals, you can go to sleep believing you had a positive day.

Visualize yourself as a success by creating a notebook in which you list the good things about your life. This project, called a Personal Book of Affirmation, is a wonderful idea I picked up from Peter J. Daniels's book *How to Be Happy Though Rich*.[5] (He's rich; I'm not.)

For my own Personal Book of Affirmation, I chose a notebook that denotes success itself: a small volume covered in top-grain leather with gilt-edged pages. I only write in it with my most expensive pen (the one I wouldn't have bought if I had known where the economy was headed). I know this is a trivial point, but it does make me feel like a success every time I read it, or pick it up to add new thoughts.

To affirm myself, I've written brief observations and memories under a variety of topical headings, including

- Accomplishments way back in high school, in college, and in business
- Good feelings about marriage, children, and extended family
- Personal achievements such as earning my pilot's license and instrument rating
- Winning awards

I've even included recollections about some of the notable people I've met, such as Vice President Hubert Humphrey, all four of the Beatles, Bob Dylan, Billy Graham, and one of the most remarkable people I've ever encountered, Corrie ten Boom, a Dutch watchmaker who, along with her family, was responsible for saving hundreds of Jews from Hitler's madness during World War II.

When I start thinking that nothing is going my way, I read a few of my handwritten pages of affirmation. It's amazing how much that helps.

The second way to build and maintain positive attitudes is to read inspirational books, such as those by Zig Ziglar, Robert Schuller, and Norman Vincent Peale. Some people think of these books as tools for sanguine personality types written by other sanguine types: "Happy Joe gives Happy Joe a little boost." But it's the melancholy personality type who needs them more than anyone. I have included a list of several of these books in the appendix.

The third tip is really simple. If you've had a bad day, don't watch the news on television before you go to bed.

End your day on positive thoughts, sounds, and images. Sometimes before we go to bed, we'll turn on a compact disc of Caribbean surf sounds and set the stereo to repeat it all night. Our Caribbean cruises and vacations have been some of our more enjoyable ones, so these sounds give us pleasant thoughts as we drift off to sleep.

The fourth tip is a crucial one: Don't hold hatred in your heart. Hate will clog your arteries and elevate your blood pressure worse than the cholesterol contained in a trainload of cheeseburgers. Medically, I have no authority to make this statement, but I know people whom hatred has destroyed.

The fifth tip to help you build positive attitudes is to be a forgiving person. Don't hold grudges. They'll eat away at you and immobilize you. Several times over the years, I've sustained significant financial losses from clients who haven't paid their bills, sticking me for tens of thousands of dollars. Later, I've come in contact with these people again. And because I had determined to be a forgiving person, I found that I could look them in the eye, offer a warm handshake, smile, and mean it. (They, on the other hand, had some difficulty with the encounter. It could have been a little problem with guilt.)

Forgiveness is not easy. It means that you have to recognize and accept the fact that people aren't perfect, that they go back on their word, and that they may not even care about you and your needs. But by being able to forgive, you will be able to focus on the concerns of your business without clogging your mind with useless thoughts and emotions.

The final tip may not apply to every reader, but if it does, I urge you to follow it. If you are a person of faith, draw upon that strength. It can help you become a forgiving person and can give you the impetus to care more deeply about others.

There will be days when you are so discouraged that none of these strategies will help. But remember, days are only days; they're not lifetimes. Tomorrow is likely to dawn brighter.

Your Knowledge

Education is an ongoing process that we all must continue long beyond the days of formal schooling if we are to compete successfully in the world of business.

One of my objectives in life is to learn something new every day. It doesn't matter whether my education takes place through reading newspapers, books or magazines, watching videos or television, listening to tapes or the radio, or engaging in stimulating conversation. I want to come to the end of each day with the realization that I have added to my mental library of useful knowledge. I need to know that I have increased my understanding of how my life, my relationships, my business, and the world at large really work.

One of the wonders of the "information age" is that we all have access to a tremendous volume of data. The task we all face is to sort through all this information to find those nuggets that will prove to be of value to us on both a personal and a business level.

One approach I use is to carry a small tape recorder or a notebook with me wherever I go. (The tape recorder is particularly useful in the car, as trying to write notes while driving could lead to sudden and unexpected air-bag deployment.) In fact, this book had its beginnings on a mini-cassette recorder that I've carried with me for years.

Another path I've followed is to clip relevant articles from newspapers or magazines, photocopy them, and place them in a ring binder labeled "Food For Thought."

It doesn't really matter how you acquire, sort, or store valuable information. Learning is always an adventure. Become an "Indiana Jones" on the quest for knowledge. Live the adventure every day!

Your Skills

The world is in a state of constant change. The skills of yesterday won't meet the demands of tomorrow. That's why it's vital to improve them—to keep pace with expanding technologies.

Just as the arc welder of yesterday must learn how to operate the computer-programmed robotic welders of today, the businessperson of today must learn how to take advantage of the advances that will lead all of us into the future.

If you've never taken a computer class, enroll in one today. If you're a little short on management skills, sign up for a good course. If you need to sharpen your writing skills, turn to a community college or nearby university.

Skills development is simply the application of new knowledge. First learn, then understand, then *do*. A growing, prospering business could be the result.

Your Courage

Although you may not think about it in this light, you had to have courage to start your own business. Many business owners leave the security of a steady paycheck to start their own companies. I did. Not only did I quit my job, but, as you know, I turned down another offer with a starting salary that I knew was substantially more than what I would make in my own business. In fact, it took me almost three years in business to equal that starting salary on a regular basis.

Courage involves making decisions, even though you could be wrong. My belief is that anyone who is confident that 51 percent of the decisions he or she makes will invariably be the right ones could easily become a multibillionaire, and could probably rule the world without much resistance from the masses.

We ordinary humans don't have it that easy. We make mistakes. But if we're afraid of making those mistakes, we will become immobilized, and our lives will screech to a boring, miserable halt.

Every day of your business life, draw from the fountain of courage you drank from when you first began your company, and you will be refreshed and invigorated.

Your Past

Many people have difficulty dealing with their pasts and blame their pasts for the problems they are experiencing in the present.

Yet, if not for your past, you wouldn't be where you are today. *Something* about your past provided you with the drive, the desire, the education, and the experiences necessary to be in business or to dream of being in business for yourself.

Naturally, the easiest path to success and prosperity would be to achieve substantial wealth through inheritance. But that seldom happens in real life. If we all inherited great fortunes, how could we ever know the satisfaction that comes through charting our own destinies, creating our own successes, conquering our own obstacles, and climbing the mountains of opportunity that life places before us?

I'm glad I never had everything handed to me. I'm grateful that my parents—who couldn't give me everything my heart desired—taught me the virtues of honesty, integrity, faith, independence, endurance, and personal drive. What a wonderful legacy for a parent to give to a child!

My past has not hurt me. It has helped me. If you give it some careful thought, you will be able to say the same thing about your past. You will, in spite of whatever pain and deprivation you've experienced, be able to point to the things that built within you the drive, the determination, and the spirit to succeed.

Your Personal Goals

As you and I begin our businesses and operate them over the years, we have little difficulty setting business goals. We draft our one-year, two-year, and five-year plans. We set sales targets and growth objectives. We create strategies for business success.

Yet, as natural as goal setting is in business, many of us think of it as out of place in our personal lives, if we think of it at all.

Of course, we all have *general* personal goals: build a new house, remodel the kitchen, buy a new car, save for the kids' college education, pay off old debts.

But we all need *specific* short-term and long-term personal goals as well—goals for which we can specifically chart our progress as we work toward them. So we don't become discouraged, our personal goals need to be realistic and attainable.

On any given day, I want to have three dreams, three personal goals, three planned events that I can anticipate with eagerness. They don't have to be big things. They can be as simple as a "date night" with my wife, an invitation to a friend's house for dinner, or a drive in the country next weekend. They could include an upcoming vacation, or tickets to the circus three months from now. The point is, I always try to have *three* things to look forward to. One or two simply aren't adequate.

The people I know who have given up on their dreams, who don't have anything special to look forward to, have, in essence, given up on living.

Apply your business principles to your personal life. Have one-year, three-year, and five-year plans for your nonbusiness self, and for your family as well.

Write them down. Find or develop some system that encourages you to prioritize your goals, and that allows you to track your progress easily and continuously. The best system I've found is the Day Planner. It can be found in office supply stores or ordered by direct mail. This system is a memory jogger that enables you to note action items in the distant future and track back to the notes you took initially, so that details don't fall through the cracks.

I carry my Day Planner with me wherever I go. I bought the largest zippered binder available—one with handles so that I can carry it like a briefcase. You would not believe what I carry in mine. In addition to the typical "diary" items such as daily calendars and phone directories, I have client files, exercise logs, credit cards, business card files, expense records, a zippered pouch for receipts, and special pockets for computer disks. You can also get city maps, graph paper, spreadsheets, a clock/calculator page divider, and my favorite—perforated, prepunched paper that I can run through my laser printer so that I can make more or less permanent records of important information, factual data, and my personal short-term and long-term goals.

The book you now hold in your hands, very candidly, was part of my three-year plan. My next book is part of my one-year plan. As I sat in my study to write, I had no idea whether anything I was writing would ever be published. Becoming a published author was merely one of my dreams, one of my goals. But I thank God that it is, because pursuing that goal is helping both my business and my personal life today.

Your Ethics

I'm amazed that my college education contributed anything to my success in life. After all, I was somewhat disadvantaged. The course offerings were so limited, so basic. I was not able to sign up for all of the "enlightened" courses being taught today. In the 1960s, I couldn't register for a course in "business ethics." Imagine that! I never had the help of a textbook—or a college professor—to help me separate right from wrong—or one shade of gray from other shades of gray, if that's how you prefer to view it.

There is black and there is white. There is wrong and there is right. There's also gray, but there's a lot less of it than most people believe.

It's been demonstrated to me again and again that the biblical edict "As you sow, so shall you reap" is an inviolable law.

I know of a company that has been in business for several decades and that once had one of the best reputations in its field. It operates in an industry where the players have exclusive representation rights for specific product lines. When the president's son graduated from college, he was brought into the business as a sales representative. Naturally (but unfortunately) he advanced within the company in leapfrog fashion, passing up other longtime loyal employees who were far more qualified for the promotions. Sadly, the son has an inflammatory personality and has actually threatened to "duke it out" with customers with whom he disagreed. He misrepresents the company's products and doesn't keep his word to anyone—vendors, customers, or employees. He is personally threatened by employees who demonstrate more knowledge of the company and its products, and has had them summarily fired on flimsy charges.

Where is he today? He's still marching toward the presidency of the company, which has discharged its most effective employees, has lost most of its longstanding product lines, and has damaged its reputation with retail stores. It will be a miracle if it survives another year. It continues to lose product lines, and its beautiful headquarters building is up for sale.

Some would say that it was simply the son's incompetence that set this disaster in motion. But I believe it was his ethics—or lack of them. He is reaping the harvest from his seeds of dishonesty.

The truly successful businessperson in today's society, the one whose success lasts, is *not* the one who lies or cheats to get ahead. The successful person follows a simple biblical principle: "Let your Yes be Yes, and let your No be No."

Mean what you say. Keep your word. Hold fast to your promises. Live up to your guarantees. Deliver the service that you sold with the product.

Our nation's courts are so overcrowded because people don't live up to their word: "I didn't really say that." "I didn't understand that contract I signed." "I don't like my old contract anymore, and if I can't have a new one, I'm going to take my football somewhere else."

Don't be on the constant lookout for "loopholes." Loopholes were invented by dishonest people to make themselves appear honest. Loopholes permit—even encourage—the manipulation of facts for improper purposes.

One standard that can't be ignored is keeping confidences. From the moment you first violate that standard, you will never be trusted again. One of the things that has amazed me for years (though it shouldn't) is that clients will tell me things well before they tell their own employees. They know that if they say, "Don't repeat this to anyone," I won't even tell my wife.

When you add up the assets of your business, you always include cash on hand, equipment, buildings, fixtures and furniture, vehicles, and inventory. But your biggest asset is missing from that list. You don't include it on your balance sheet because it has no easily determined market value. In fact, it's impossible to attach a dollar amount to it. That asset is your reputation. Guard it. Protect it. Never let it become a liability.

You've heard the old adage, "Don't get mad, get even." Over the short term, that philosophy may prove workable. But it certainly doesn't fit with an even older teaching, "Don't repay evil with evil, but repay evil with good."

This is tough advice to follow. It runs contrary to everything most of us have been taught—"Only the strong survive"; "You have to be tough to play this game"; "Don't let 'em walk all over you."

There is room for kindness in business. There are businesspeople who play the game by the highest standards and who still win. It's definitely worth a try.

Your Support System

When the difficulties of being in business for yourself drag you down, don't try to make it through your problems on your own. Don't be afraid to utter a cry for help. Find a support group, or a variety of support groups, and welcome them into your life.

Your first line of defense in a nonsense economy and a crazy world should be your *family*. I can arrive home from what I believe has been the worst day of my life, and the hugs from my kids can erase it all. My wife and I can sit down to a beautiful dinner, and suddenly, slow receivables cease to exist. We can pick up the phone and call our parents—none of whom has ever been an independent businessperson—and they seem to understand, care, and affirm.

Your *friends* should come right behind your family. Be willing to reveal your thoughts, feelings, fears, and dreams to friends who care. My male readers will undoubtedly believe they understand the notion of male bonding, yet they would never reveal their fears, frustrations, questions, or problems to someone with whom they play poker or watch Monday night football. Male bonding to them means that you do "guy stuff" together—sports, hunting, or fishing. I believe that women have a better notion of what friendship really is and should be. While all people conceal certain aspects of who they are and what aspirations they have, women are more willing to reveal their thoughts and feelings, fears, and dreams.

Your third source of support can be *organized small groups*, from recovery/therapy groups to clubs and special-interest organizations to nondenominational Bible studies.

Professional counselors can also be of tremendous support and benefit. Years ago, anyone who saw a psychiatrist or other professional was viewed as suspect. Today, the stigma associated with counseling has, for the most part, vanished. Counselors can help sort through a variety of personal, marital, family, and professional matters. Career counselors can help with the decision about whether to change direction in life, and business counselors might be able to provide that one gem of truth that can get a troubled business back on track.

Professional and religious retreats have gained great acceptance and are becoming more readily available. In many of these settings, because the participants may not have met previously, they open up more willingly. In other types of retreats, the focus may be on quiet and meditation. Also popular are marital retreats, where couples are able to enhance their marriages.

Churches and synagogues often provide free or low-cost counseling, recovery groups, and other supportive services. I have known many priests, pastors, and rabbis over the years who exhibit a deep caring not only for those in their congregations but also for those who simply call in times of need. They are able to bring fresh insight to a wide range of questions and problems.

The key to developing an effective support system is that you have to want to seek help. Seldom will a support person or group come looking for you.

9

YOUR EMPLOYEES

If I could operate a successful, growing, multibillion-dollar business without employees, I would. They whine, they call in sick, they go on vacation at the most inconvenient times, they take long lunches, they want raises, they demand more benefits, they leave without notice, and when they leave they try to take your best clients with them.

It's impossible to keep every employee happy all of the time. All have different needs, interests, goals, aspirations, fears, and demands. Rarely do they all get along with each other. They're jealous and petty. They form alliances among themselves to try to get the better of you. They want to work less and get paid more. Make one false move, and they'll try to form a labor union or drag you into court.

But almost without exception, employees are a necessary part of doing business. More than that—they're the lifeblood of your business. Without them, you have no one to make, sell, or distribute your product. There is no one to install and maintain your equipment, no one to collect your receivables and pay your bills, no one to service your customers or relay your messages.

This is all pitifully obvious. But many businesses that are in trouble got there because they overlooked the value and importance of their employees. Good employees are on the same level as loyal customers and dependable vendors: They are among your most valuable assets.

The reverse is also true. Incompetent employees, like fickle clients and undependable vendors, are among your greatest liabilities.

A rude employee can turn your customer into someone else's customer with a "don't bother me" attitude toward a question. Until I had a candid talk with one of my employees about phone manners, several of my longtime customers had asked me, "Who is that angry-sounding person who answered the phone?" There is no place for rudeness in a successful business.

The unproductive employee can be demoralizing to the rest of your employees. They will naturally wonder why someone who doesn't produce gets paid as much as (or sometimes more than) the employee who gives it her or his all.

If we are to maintain any degree of competitiveness in the global economy, American businesses must return to the basics of quality and value. We must strive for excellence. With that in mind, I have developed a model for my own business that will be operative throughout my second start-up phase. Called the Quest for Excellence, it is built on a program of accountability and rewards.

The Quest for Excellence

In 1992, the *Minneapolis Star Tribune* reported the story of a Chicago man whose commercial building construction business hit the recession skids and eventually went under.[6] Several months later, the Chicago Sheraton Hotel ran an ad for menial labor positions. The former $40,000-a-year business owner stood in line with 9,000 other applicants and was ultimately chosen over the others to fill a position as a $200 per week custodian who cleans bathrooms. He was thrilled to get that job, and he says he takes tremendous pride in his work.

I recount this story for two reasons. First, I do not want to be in that man's position—*ever*. Second, I want to remind my employees of the hard reality that in a recessionary economy, nothing is for sure. A recessionary economy intensifies competition, as companies fight over the few remaining pieces of a smaller pie. Only when management and employees work together in a quest for excellence can they have the power to successfully fight the ravages of recession.

Although I don't believe in perfection, because, realistically, it can never be attained, I do believe in the *quest* for excellence. I believe in improving our product in every way possible and continually striving to be better at everything we do.

The quest for excellence should be formalized in every company's culture and ethic, under whatever phrase or word the company chooses to use. The objectives of this program should be fourfold. It should

- Nurture quality work
- Build commitment to one another
- Assure accountability
- Reward top performance

Nurture Quality Work

Companies that stay alive and prosper will be run by people who foster and expect quality work from their employees. The business owners will recognize that, as competition for every dollar becomes more fierce, they have to offer a better product at a lower (or more efficient) price.

In our business, we are aware that other ad agencies and video companies are calling on our accounts and our prospects every day of the business week. They are telling these clients and potential clients that they can do better work (quality) at a lower, or more efficient cost (value), with better results (profits). The minute that one of our clients believes these claims, we will no longer have the client. If a prospect believes the claims, we won't have a viable prospect.

As a businessperson, you know that quality is crucial. Quality means doing things right. But it also encompasses value and generates results.

In the advertising realm, quality may not necessarily mean that the most splendid design is executed by the most expensive color separator and printed by the most expensive printer. Quality *does* mean that the job is completed within budget, that it fulfills its intended function, and that the job is error-free. Errors signal to the client that no one cares, that attention to detail is sloppy, and that there must be someone out there who can do it better—and do it right.

Build Commitment to One Another

Another characteristic common to successful companies is teamwork. To achieve top quality, everyone on the team must fulfill his or her role, rather than trying to redefine those roles to fit their personal interests.

Great assembly line workers can't build great cars unless those cars are based on great designs. The designers must be committed to designing great cars. The machinists must be committed to executing great tools, dies, and molds. The assembly line workers must be dedicated to using those tools and dies in the ways they were designed to be used. And the inspectors who sign off on the completed automobiles must observe the high standards they are intended to follow.

On a professional football team, each player has been hired to fulfill a specific set of assignments. If those assignments are met, the team wins. If those assignments are blown, the team loses. Players who blow their assignments are traded or cut from the team. Players who fulfill their assignments get a shot at the playoffs. And when the team wins the Super Bowl, every member of the team gets a bonus.

For a "business team" to survive in the 1990s, coaches will have to insist that assignments not be blown. They will have to make cuts if the team is losing. They will have to sign proven performers.

As a result of the losses my company sustained, we made some necessary cuts on the team. The team had been losing. We had no other choice.

Today and tomorrow, as we rebuild, we will do everything possible to sign proven performers, so that every season can be a winning season. Every competitive company must be willing to do the same.

Assure Accountability

You must have some means to measure quality in the broadest sense, and that means setting some standards. Until recently, our company had never had specific standards for our work, other than "Do your best." Today, it is essential that we establish minimum standards for our own on-the-job performance and for new people we bring on staff. With realistic guidelines, each person will be held accountable for meeting those standards.

Reward Top Performance

Although I used a football analogy to illustrate a point earlier, there is one practice in the world of the NFL that I don't like. And that is, if a team wins the Super Bowl, all the players get the same winner's share and the same jewel-encrusted ring, whether they played the entire game or never set foot on the field.

While this type of reward promotes teamwork, it does nothing for the players who give everything they've got, even at the risk of pain, injury, and possibly even an end to their careers.

I believe that companies should reward top performers and not automatically give the winner's share and gold ring to every "player" simply because he or she showed up. In the past, some of our company's players would show up on "game day" but had forgotten their uniforms or were hobbling along on crutches. Yet we gave them the same rewards as the players who came to the game fully prepared and eager to play. Why can't we develop a clearly defined system to reward people based on their performance, without violating all of the antidiscrimination laws on the books?

One of my problems with labor unions is that they encourage low levels of productivity. Their system of rewards is based not on output but on longevity—everyone receives the same level of pay and the same benefits based on such meaningless criteria as seniority. Similarly, I think tenure is the real reason that there are so many poor-quality teachers in our public school systems. There's no way to get rid of them.

I am an advocate of equal pay for equal work. A woman who does the same work as a man should receive equal pay—without question, without objection. A woman who outperforms her male counterparts should get *more* pay—without question, without objection.

If you have fulfilled your ethical and moral responsibility to give every employee an equal opportunity to succeed, without regard to race, creed, or sex, you should have the right to discriminate on matters of salaries, bonuses, and promotions, based on measurable performance. You should be able to do so without fear of litigation, but the days when you can do so are passing quickly.

The Drive for Profits

In the successful business of the 1990s, every employee must buy into the premise that profits are everyone's concern. And profits are generally based on productivity—both on the manufacturing and distribution side and on the sales and management side.

Jobs can exist only if profits exist. Pay increases can be given only when there is an increase in the available amount of money—in a word, profits. But management cannot be held solely responsible for profits. A major part of the responsibility rests with the employees. In the real world of business, your employees are as responsible for their own paychecks as you, the owner, are. It's time that message became clear. You didn't necessarily go into business to guarantee your employees a job. You went into business and hired employees so that you could guarantee a job for yourself. You can't afford to carry dead weight.

Building Morale

Advertising is a highly subjective field. As one of the primary account executives for our company, I interact frequently with our clients. And I can tell you that clients are more prone to criticize than to praise, even when we're doing an outstanding job and their sales are increasing dramatically. Advertising is simply our job, we're getting paid for it, and we're expected to do it well—praise or not.

Because I have received so little positive affirmation for my work over the years, I have not valued praise as much as I should, and I have been slow to praise my employees for their contributions. In fact, when I've hired people in the past, I've said in their final interview, "I don't get much praise, so I don't dish much out, either. Don't take that to mean you're not doing a good job, though."

Well, folks, this is not a philosophy on which great companies are built. It leads to lackluster performance and job dissatisfaction. It is vital that every employer develop a strategy for building the morale of individuals as well as the company as a whole.

The three most direct tactics for building employee morale are to (1) praise quality work, (2) build camaraderie and a spirit of teamwork, and (3) create an environment in which people know that they will be rewarded for their contributions and will be afforded the opportunity for advancement.

Praise Quality Work

Praise, of course, is easier to lavish on employees who are actually doing a good job. But one crucial truth I've learned from being the father of three children is that everyone needs praise, and there is always something for which every person deserves praise. It may be a stretch. You may have to dig a little to find something. But it can be found.

I'm reminded of a story about a schoolteacher placed in charge of a group of underachievers and learning disabled students—without that fact being made clear to her at the time. After these kids had spent a year in her class, the principal came to her and said, "I can't believe the progress you're making with your students. They're performing as well as their counterparts in the mainstream classes." The teacher, with a look of disbelief, responded, "Why shouldn't they? Just look at their IQ scores: 126, 142, 138, 123. They're all quite bright! Some are even in the genius category." The principal examined her list more closely. "Those aren't their IQs," he said. "Those are their *locker numbers.*" As this story illustrates, if you have high expectations, there's a good chance they'll be met.

A word of caution: Employees are capable of detecting false praise. The employee you're praising, and others within earshot, will know whether or not your words are genuine. Don't try to fake it.

Your words of affirmation should follow two paths. Some should be spoken in private, directly to the employee. Some should be in public, to foster recognition and acceptance. Just make sure that one employee isn't singled out for the bulk of your public encouragement.

With our energetic, fun-loving new team in place, we've taken to such nonbusinesslike notions as applauding employees in our Monday morning staff meetings. Some seem to be embarrassed, some take bows, but they all love it. Every human being thrives on recognition.

Build Camaraderie

Your company can use a variety of approaches to build camaraderie and a spirit of teamwork. Your initial response to some of my company's tactics may be, "Well, that works in ad agencies because they're nothing but a bowl of creative flakes in the first place." You may be right, but try these on for size.

- If we get a piece of good news, no matter how great or small, we ring the "good news bell" that hangs in our lobby. One gong is small news, two gongs means bigger news, and so on. (The record is twenty-seven, I think.)

In these uncertain times, we ring the bell whenever there's money in the morning mail. We ring the bell when we get a new order from an existing client. And we nearly ring the bell off the wall when we get a new client. (We discovered, quite by accident, that one of our larger but more fun-loving clients had hung a similar bell, at about the same time, for the same purpose. That company is so well run and is growing so successfully that its bell must be ringing all the time!)

- Every two or three weeks, we schedule Hat Day or Tie Day or Boot Day or Sweatshirt Day. We all include the specifically named item in our work outfit of the day. After work, we go out as a group for a couple of hours to snack on appetizers and talk about "life" at a local restaurant. In rotation, every employee has the opportunity to determine the theme and select the destination.

- Instead of commemorating Secretary's Day or Secretary's Week (which this aging conservative considers horribly sexist), we observe Employee Appreciation Week during the same general time period. Every employee receives a potted "mini-garden" designed by a local florist, along with the afternoon off and lunch at a waterfront restaurant.

- Every May, depending on the level of interest, we hold a company golf tournament, complete with trophies for "high gross" and "most putts." Okay, so we're not serious golfers.

- For a number of years, our company has observed Martin Luther King, Jr. Day as an official holiday. Because January is always cold and snow-covered in Minnesota, we schedule a ski outing for the staff. At the end of the day, we raise our mugs of hot apple cider to the memory of a man who gave millions of people a reason to have dreams to call their own.

Create an Environment of Opportunity

Of the three tactics for building morale, the most important is to create an environment in which people know that they will be rewarded for their contributions and will have an opportunity for advancement. The most common and accepted way to reward an employee's contributions is through a raise or a promotion. Raises are dependent, of course, on profits. Promotions that involve a new title don't cost anything if the only reward is the title itself—Vice President, Sales, for example. But for a title to be anything other than a gesture, it should be linked to a pay increase. Your employees will quickly see through shallow ploys designed solely to keep them happy.

At The Gottry Group, we believe in promoting from within, creating opportunity for the people who already work for us. One person who started as a receptionist became our media director in a very short time—thanks to demonstrated interest, tremendous proficiency, and a strong desire for career advancement. It was truly a well-deserved reward, accompanied by a pay increase.

There are other rewards that, in the long term, cost less than a raise but can have almost as much positive impact. Sales contests are one example. The promise of a Caribbean cruise or a trip to Hawaii can increase the productivity of your entire sales department.

Because we're currently on a tight budget, my top salesperson, Karla, came up with the idea of "time out" coupons. Members of the staff who have been putting in extra-long hours or who have done something above and beyond the call of duty are awarded a gift certificate valid at a local restaurant, so they can take a "time out."

It is less important *how* you recognize employees than the fact that you *do* recognize them. Employees who are praised, encouraged, promoted, and rewarded are more likely to care, be productive, and remain with the company.

Setting Expectations

If an employee is ineffective on the job, it is often because he or she has not been properly trained, does not know what his or her employer's expectations are, and isn't corrected when standards aren't met.

As an employer, you must clearly and continually state your expectations to every employee. You must make certain everyone understands the company's goals, procedures, products, and services.

Communicating these things only one time won't do. Until recently, I had always assumed otherwise. "People are bright, receptive, and pay close attention," I've said to myself. "They'll catch on right away, and I won't have to repeat anything twice."

Wrong.

If I've learned anything as the result of being in the advertising business, it's that *frequency*—repeating the same message over and over to the same audience—is the key to building brand recognition, being remembered by the consumer, and delivering results in the form of sales. Your employees are the "consumers" of your company's policies, procedures, goals, standards, and philosophies.

They need to be told, told again, reminded, reinforced, and reminded again. They need to buy into everything about the company.

Be direct. Set goals. Teach your people to be good representatives of your company—to care about customers, to help each other, to be a team.

But make sure they're ready to play on the team. Don't expect your employees to deliver miracles if they don't have sufficient experience or if you haven't provided adequate training. Can you imagine a scenario wherein a professional football coach assembles a team of men who have never exercised in their lives, who have never touched a football, who don't know the basic rules of American football, and then expects to turn them into Super Bowl champions their first season? It wouldn't matter how great the coach is, it just won't happen. But if that same coach could pick the best players from every other NFL team, work them hard, and teach them how to execute every play flawlessly, they'd have a better-than-average shot at those Super Bowl rings.

Good players cost money. Effective training programs cost money. With employees—as with anything else in life—you will never get something for nothing.

When you have assembled a team of eager, experienced, trained employees, you can set the highest standards and expect your employees to meet them.

The Job Description

Every employee should know what tasks he or she will be asked to fulfill and what standards will be used to judge performance. This objective is best met through a combination of the employee handbook and a job description. My approach is to provide a detailed handbook that provides basic minimum standards with regard to working hours, company policies, and general expectations. (The handbook's contents are outlined in Chapter 2.) The job description provides information on specific duties and outlines reporting procedures and supervisory responsibilities.

A well-drawn job description should not limit the employee's growth or suppress his or her imagination or eagerness, nor should it describe specific procedures in detail. The latter function is best left to procedural memos, meetings, or handbooks. Instead, it should paint a larger picture of the basic areas in which the employee can contribute to the overall success of the company.

The first page of each of our job descriptions outlines the following:

1. Job title
2. General nature of the position (full or part time; salaried, hourly, or commissioned; union or non-union; any limitation on benefits the company will provide)
3. To whom the employee reports
4. Who reports to the employee
5. Pay range for the position

The rest of the job description outlines the employee's general responsibilities. It does not concentrate on specifics; rather, it encourages both freedom and involvement. An example of a job description at our company is presented on the following page.

In every job description, from receptionist to vice president, from media coordinator to copy writer, we stress that the job is a *team position*. A key concept deeply ingrained in our company's culture is: "If there's a job to be done, and you're in the best position to do it, then do it."

The creative director will

1. *Create*. Participate in regular and unscheduled meetings to develop creative strategies for clients and for specific projects. Focus on combining headlines and copy with illustrations and design to communicate a strong, integrated sales message.

2. *Innovate*. Seek out and identify new, fresh, innovative ways to solve advertising/marketing problems, and, when possible, apply them on our clients' behalf.

3. *Estimate*. Work with account people to develop "doable" budgets. Judge the amount of creative time and add costs for outside services to provide a realistic estimate to clients. Communicate and store this information on meaningful forms for quick retrieval. Contribute to profits by seeing to it that budgets are not exceeded.

4. *Delegate*. Assign tasks to the persons with the best skills and most available time to suitably handle the job. Use staff people first before assigning jobs to freelancers.

5. *Communicate*. State objectives, target budgets, and a clear outline of the job to be done to others in the creative department. Relay goals, concerns, and problems to the president.

Figure 3. Sample Job Description: Creative Director

Communicate positive and healthy attitudes to other staff members, and be a leader. Don't let bad ideas from others stop you from pushing for the best solutions. Make sure that communication is multilevel, multichannel, two-way, and "on the table."

6. *Facilitate.* Make it possible for others to better do their jobs, so that duplicated steps and wasted time are eliminated. By using others' time more effectively, you will use your own time more effectively.

7. *Educate.* Teach others what you know— about computers, type, design, printing, procedures, management, life.

8. *Generate.* Create excitement, ideas, and profits by fostering a spirit of cooperation, teamwork, openness, and enthusiasm toward the agency, its clients, and its creative product.

9. *Cooperate.* Work with your supervisor, with other staff members, and with clients and suppliers so that we can produce advertising and collateral materials that make a difference.

10. *Recreate.* Have fun in your off hours, and take time during the busiest work week to break for recreation or an occasional long lunch. After all, "seriousity killed the cat."

Figure 3. Sample Job Description: Creative Director (continued)

While these categories are specific to certain jobs within the context of an advertising agency, they can serve as the foundation for job descriptions in any industry—if one of the underlying goals is to create both independence and interdependence and both freedom and responsibility in the workplace.

The Nonperformer

It hurts to be forced by economic conditions to let an employee who is performing well go. It's a little easier—though not much—to dismiss employees because they have failed to perform as expected or required.

It's important that you carefully document employee performance, so that if you dismiss someone, you have adequate support material to back you up. One reason I'm an advocate of employee handbooks and written job descriptions is that they can provide the basis for an objective judgment of performance.

I have had my share of nonperformers, including an alcoholic who seldom returned from lunch; an account executive who claimed to be out on calls when, in fact, many afternoons were spent horseback riding; and a person who spent nearly a third of the workday on personal phone calls.

Nonperformers can be replaced by people who truly want to contribute. You owe it to your loyal, caring, hardworking employees to replace them. If you keep them on the payroll with the hope of somehow rehabilitating them, you'll only drag your company down.

The Disgruntled Employee

Throughout the life of my business, especially during the more profitable years, I have given my employees nearly everything you could imagine: early raises; expense accounts; heated indoor parking; gift certificates in appreciation of extra effort; medical reimbursement payments for out-of-pocket health care expenses; tuition reimbursement for college courses they wanted to take; fully paid life, health, and disability insurance; holiday bonuses; "arts" reimbursements (we paid for their concert and theater tickets, which was reported as additional income); golf tournaments and ski outings. If you can name it, we probably did it. (But not today.)

My philosophy was, "Take good care of your employees, and they'll take good care of you." Some will, and some won't. I've discovered that if you offer your employees the moon, they'll be only too happy to take it.

While some employees will appreciate your kindnesses and considerations, others will turn on you no matter what you do for them. They will bad-mouth you, reveal your trade secrets, and probably go to work for your toughest competitor. I realize this sounds cynical, but it's still a fact.

When an employee's attitude turns sour, you can only hope that you haven't committed some unpardonable sin that could land you in court. If you want to avoid this situation, here is some important advice to follow:

1. Don't create a hostile, uncomfortable, unhealthful, or sexist workplace, and don't allow those who work for you to do so.
2. Don't do anything that could be construed as discriminatory against any person or group of persons.

3. Keep accurate, up-to-date personnel files, and make sure that you have proof of cause for every disciplinary action you take.

4. Make sure your employees receive equal pay for equal work.

5. Follow the letter of the law with regard to the employment practices that apply in your state.

6. Don't put anything in writing that may come back to haunt you. For example, don't write a positive performance review for an employee with whom you are having difficulties.

7. Make sure your lawyer has the opportunity to review your practices and procedures on a regular basis. Laws change, even if your policies don't.

If you violate any of these principles, there's a fair chance that, in today's litigious atmosphere, you will face your disgruntled former employee in court.

The Employee Who Would Be Boss

Every company eventually employs someone who thinks he or she should be the boss. Such people try to control you. They test you. They push the limits.

They control meetings by coming late, leaving early, exhibiting poor attitudes, or acting distracted. Believe it or not, I *had* an employee who would actually decide for himself when a meeting I had called should be over and would walk out, saying he had important things to do. He did so in spite of the fact that I always try to keep our meetings as short as possible. The same individual would tell my other employees to go against my direct instructions, under the premise that his approach was far better.

This kind of employee will test you to see whether you really follow your own policies. Often, such people think of their contributions as indispensable, and they will nudge the boundaries to see how far you'll let them go.

Your employees have to know that while you will examine all the hands they play, the high card (you) always wins. Yes, you're interested in fresh new ideas. Yes, you appreciate helpful suggestions. But no matter what you've heard to the contrary, successful companies simply can't be run by a committee. Certain aspects can be (for example, new business development committees can be extremely productive), but ultimately, the boss has to make the most crucial decisions.

I'm not advocating that you become a dictator who won't listen to reason or who summarily dismisses employees who express a differing opinion. Once you have made a decision, though, your employees are obligated to stand behind you. When they don't, you have a problem.

To prepare for the inevitable outcome of confrontation—termination of the employee—make sure you have maintained documentation of his or her questionable actions, hostilities, and insubordination or covert plans. If an employee has fought you for control, generally that strong-willed determination will surface again, under the worst of circumstances.

Building Successful Relationships With Employees

Your relationship with your employees is partly a formal contract and partly a mutual understanding that should benefit both of you equally. It all distills down to what you owe your employees, and what they owe you.

Copy

Seven Things You Owe Your Employees

You owe your employees

1. A regular, on-time paycheck
2. A safe working environment
3. Adequate insurance to protect them from loss as the result of catastrophic illness
4. Benefits (vacations, holidays, sick leave, retirement plans) in keeping with industry standards
5. A reward system based on performance
6. An equal and fair opportunity for advancement, without regard to race, sex, religion, or any other discriminatory factor
7. Respect for their ideas, their suggestions, and their aspirations

Seven Things Your Employees Owe You

Your employees owe you

1. An honest day's work for an honest day's pay. (This means keeping personal phone calls to a minimum, actively seeking ways to make meaningful contributions, performing tasks with a high degree of accuracy, reporting for work on time, and not watching the clock for the entire last hour of the day.)
2. Full-time loyalty
3. Respect for confidential information
4. Integrity and honesty in all dealings that represent the company
5. Respect for you, the employer, and for their fellow employees

6. A positive attitude on the job

7. Courtesy toward the company's clients, vendors, and competitors

If each party, employer and employee, can deliver on this very basic list, together you will have laid the foundation for building a successful company. And as the employer, you will be maximizing one of your most valuable assets.

10

YOUR CUSTOMERS AND VENDORS

There are only two kinds of customers: satisfied and dissatisfied. The satisfied customer will generally result in a repeat sale or a continuing relationship; the dissatisfied customer usually will not.

There's a reason I qualify this statement with the words *generally* and *usually*. For example, if you're a real estate broker who sells a family their dream house, they may never come back to you with repeat business, even though they have been completely satisfied with your service. Conversely, if you're the only supplier of a product or service in a defined market, you may get repeat business from disgruntled customers simply because they have no other convenient choice.

Taking Care of Your Customers

However, customer satisfaction or dissatisfaction impacts more than just repeat sales. Customers are often your most widespread and believable form of advertising. They use the medium called word of mouth, and there are only two kinds of word of mouth: good and bad.

If you were entirely responsible for your relationships with your customers, you would probably enjoy tremendous and ongoing success. All of your word-of-mouth advertising would be positive. After all, who understands the value of customers more clearly than the owner of the company?

But your employees also enter into the relationships with your customers, and they can have a profound impact on how customer service at your company is perceived. It's vital that you never disparage your customers in the presence of your employees—no matter how irritating or unprofessional those customers may be. Negative attitudes and comments always seem to get back to the customer.

You are responsible for teaching your employees that it is the *customer*, not you, who pays their salaries and keeps the company in business. *They* are the reason your employees are employed.

You are the one who must instill in each and every employee the paramount importance of quality customer service. Without service, your customers will become your competitor's customers.

The Nationwide Lack of Customer Service

We hear much talk about the fact that the United States is, or is becoming, a "service-based" economy. If that is indeed the case, we are in for serious trouble. Unless there are major changes in the ways companies operate, we are doomed to become a second-class nation.

My wife and I recently observed that we have to do everything twice. Here's what we mean.

Illustration number one: It's been a hectic day, so we decide to ignore our low-fat diet just for today and go to the fast-food drive-through window. We ordered three cheeseburgers, two fries, three sodas, and one Jolly Meal for our four-year-old. We drive all the way home and discover that there are no fries and that the free plastic toy that is supposed to come with the Jolly Meal is missing. So we drive back, wait in line, and eventually pick up the rest of our order. We've had to drive through that line twice.

Illustration number two: We drive to the "Speedy Oil Change" location near us to get a quick oil and filter change. *After* we've driven onto the ramp and the mechanics have drained the old oil, they discover that they're out of filters for our minivan. Guess what? We have to make a return trip. (We also switch to the competition for future oil changes.)

Illustration number three: While shopping one day, we come across an imported Italian espresso machine on sale. We both love espresso and cappuccino, so we buy it—factory fresh, in a sealed carton. We get home, unpack it, and discover that the directions are missing. So it's back to the store for instructions.

Illustration number four: We decide to buy two matching office chairs for our office at home, so we trudge off to the local outlet of a national office supply chain. We select our chairs, pay for them, and wait for a nice young man to bring them to our minivan. They are in boxes. But by now we have become a little smarter. "We'd like to open the boxes to make sure they're the right ones," we say. "Oh, they are," says he. "I pulled them from stock myself." "Just the same..." Sure enough, one is black, and one is mauve with tan and teal flecks.

We now check every drive-through meal, every order, and every carton before we bring it home. We verify every delivery before we accept it. And we try on every new suit that's gone through alterations before we leave the store.

We are forced to do this because customer service has become unbelievably sloppy and attention to detail has been nearly eradicated by employees who do not comprehend the simple principle that it is the customers who pay their salary, hourly wages, or commission.

A few years back, I stumbled across a book titled *How to Win Customers and Keep Them for Life*, by Michael LeBoeuf.[7] After reading it, I went back to the store, bought a dozen copies, and essentially forced my employees to read it. They took turns serving as discussion leaders on the content of this book during our Monday morning staff meetings. The book is now mandatory reading for every new employee of our company, and I could not recommend it more highly.

I have just recently discovered another, equally valuable book, *Customers for Life*, by Carl Sewell and Paul B. Brown.[8] As helpful as both these books are, I hope you aren't misled into believing that if you follow the authors' principles to the letter you will seldom lose a customer or client. Despite all the solid advice, *the truth is that customer loyalty does not really exist.*

People can and do develop loyalties toward other *people*. Occasionally, they may become truly loyal to a particular *brand*. But they are seldom, if ever, loyal to a *company*. A company is nothing more than a name on a door. It is hardly ever perceived as something that possesses a "personality."

In Chapter 4, I offered my view of how value is judged in times of recession. Quality, I said, takes a backseat to price in the customer's determination of the value of any product or service. In a down economy and the period that follows it, nearly every customer is looking for the deal. While some may still place a high priority on quality, most shop price.

Someone once said, "You can always find someone to produce it a little cheaper and do it a little worse." Today, *cheaper* and *worse* seem to be acceptable alternatives to *more expensive* and *better*. The company that seeks to maintain its standards in producing top-quality goods and services will be forced to maintain or even raise prices in order to make a profit and may find itself coming up short on customer loyalty.

As an example, the people in our video division have consistently demonstrated that they are willing to put in extra effort to produce a superior product at a fair price. Yet we are losing jobs to other companies that produce a poor product on a low budget. Does it matter that the quality is shoddy? Does it matter that the video is devoid of any meaningful or convincing sales message? Does it matter that anyone who receives the video is likely to watch only a few seconds of the program? Apparently not.

The highest level of customer service in the world often will not win out over the customer's perceived need to "get it cheap."

Karla and I have spent substantial amounts of time and money to build relationships with our clients. We have invited them to nights on the town—dinner, theater, concerts. We have taken them boating, golfing, and flying. We have shown a genuine interest in them: we've sent gifts when they've given birth, or flowers or memorials when a relative has died. Our interest and concern are genuine. We really do care. And we enjoy our relationships with our customers.

Yet, time and time again, we have seen these relationships evaporate without warning. In one case, it was over an estimate that was a few dollars higher than an upstart competitor's. In another case, it was the result of a customer's new employee assuming an increasing role in the decision-making process; he brought in an agency with whom he had an established relationship. In a recent case, it was simply our nonsense economy. Quality was less important that the need to save money by performing the work in-house.

Times of Vulnerability

There are certain times when your company is at its most vulnerable—when your relationships with your customers are the most at risk:

1. When the customer's "buyer" changes. This one has affected us time and time again. The advertising manager or marketing director with whom we have worked leaves, and the new buyer brings in a team of people with whom she or he is comfortable. Naturally, we try to build a relationship with the new person, but it doesn't always work.

2. When the customer's owner changes. New owners, of course, bring their former relationships with them, and since they're the boss...

3. When the customer's needs change and you are unable to meet the new requirements. You've theoretically been watching trends and have been able to respond quickly enough to the changing needs of your customers, but sometimes their needs change quickly and unexpectedly, and it may not be practical or profitable for you to respond.

4. When a new business offering a similar product or service is able to compete with you directly. For example, if you run a neighborhood grocery store and a new megasupermarket opens its doors two blocks away, your customers will probably give them a try.

5. When you make a mistake. Your customers can't afford to lose money or be placed in an awkward position with *their* customers as the result of your errors or omissions.

6. When you fail to deliver as promised. Your customers don't want excuses—they want what they want, when they want it. (A few months ago, we obtained a new client who placed several orders with us. Because of a number of factors that *we* felt were legitimate—including a major hard drive crash on our computer—we delivered a number of assignments late. The client was justifiably upset, and we are doing everything possible to salvage the relationship. Only time will tell.)

7. When the economy makes price the most important factor. It bears repeating that in an uncertain economy, if you can't compete on price, you probably can't compete.

This can also work in reverse. These same times of vulnerability may also provide the best opportunity to win new customers away from your competitors.

Keeping customers—and keeping them satisfied—in the volatile 1990s will be a challenge for nearly every small business. For that reason, businesspeople will be forced to place an increased emphasis on acquiring a steady stream of new prospects and new customers. They will need to evaluate and improve their service, develop a competitive pricing strategy, and adapt their products or services to meet the changing needs and tastes of the customer.

There's only one way to play the game today: *value your customers, treat them fairly, serve them well*. They are one of your most important business assets.

Dealing With Your Vendors

In general, all business involves buying something (raw materials or the services of employees), doing something to it (fabricating it, merchandising it, or creating something of value from it), and selling it for more than you paid for it. As the first step of this process, most businesses have to work with vendors or outside suppliers.

Vendors are a vital link in the business chain, yet I've known business owners and managers who treat their vendors as though they represent the lowest form of prehistoric life. They are demanding, demeaning, overbearing, and unforgiving and act as though they could live without the very people who provide the goods and services that keep them in business.

The minute some other vendor walks through these manager's doors with a price that is a few cents lower, they will toss aside their relationship with their longtime supplier and switch loyalties—if you could call it that.

I've known other business owners and managers who have treated their vendors with the respect accorded to true partners. They are understanding, patient, supportive, and trusting. Of course, they expect good service and fair pricing, but they also reward outstanding performance through loyalty and friendship.

These managers realize that it is vital that their vendors make a profit. Suppliers that are not in a solid financial position cannot provide the levels of service and support, nor the timeliness of delivery, that these astute managers expect. Price pressure can also lead to the lowering of manufacturing standards, and an inferior product from a vendor will ultimately lower the quality of the end product or service.

Naturally, healthy and beneficial relationships between your company and your suppliers must be built on a foundation of trust. You have an obligation to be loyal to those who have served your needs in an effective and timely manner. You owe it to them to make your expectations clear yet reasonable and to allow them to make a fair profit. For their part, your suppliers have an obligation to set fair, competitive prices, to keep you informed on the status of your order, and to do everything within their power to deliver a product that meets or exceeds your specifications—on time.

The relationship between your company and your vendors can be summed up in a few simple "fair trade practices."

Seven Guidelines for Vendors

Vendors should try to follow these principles:

1. Realize that a successful business is built on the foundation of many customers who each have a role in that success. Don't try to make all your profit from one customer. Treat your small customers as though they are as important as your big customers. They are.

2. Deliver a product or service that meets or exceeds the specifications of your customers.

3. Deliver it on time.

4. Keep your customers informed about any problems that may affect price, quality, or delivery schedules. Nobody likes surprises, except on their birthdays.

5. Pass any unexpected savings you realize along to your customer. It will build loyalty and create goodwill. Ultimately, it will help you fend off your competitors who may have already found the key to the delivery of a better product at a lower price.

6. Let your word be as binding as written contracts.

7. Appreciate your loyal customers. By this, I don't mean try to buy them off. But remember what's

important to them. If they love golf, drop your business for an afternoon and spend time with them. Help them out with their favorite community service project. *Tell* them you appreciate their business.

Seven Guidelines for Customers

In dealing with vendors, customers should try to follow these principles:

1. Set reasonable expectations—make reasonable demands.

2. Don't try to beat your vendors down on price. Recognize that they must make a fair profit to remain in business.

3. Don't change the rules in midstream. Do not expect more than you bargained for, or change pricing or delivery schedules after the fact.

4. Don't drop a faithful supplier for insignificant or arbitrary reasons. Everyone makes mistakes. The mature customer makes allowances for the occasional mistake.

5. If possible, pay your vendors within their terms, and don't attempt to negotiate new terms of your own. (Don't pay them earlier than their terms require, however, for reasons covered in Chapter 11).

6. Let your word be as binding as your written contracts.

7. Appreciate your vendors. Don't take them for granted. For more than twenty years, we've had a vendor who has served many of our graphic production needs. In 1974 we gave this vendor, who had never missed one of our deadlines, a

simple engraved plaque, "Lightning Award," on which we added the words, "To the great people who know the meaning of the word 'Rush.'" In all the years since that award was presented, they've *still* never missed a deadline for us.

The relationship between you and your vendors should not be adversarial. You're in this thing together. Without customers, there would be no vendors. And without vendors, virtually no companies would exist. There will never be a time, in any nation or any economy, when one giant company will meet all the needs of all the people. The world will always revolve around buying and selling. There will always be business... as usual!

11

YOUR CAPITAL

Thousands of books have been written about money—how to acquire it, manage it, control it, invest it, and retire on it. You could learn a great deal from these books. However, what every small-business owner needs to know about capital can be summarized into seven basic rules:.

1. Move it in your door as quickly as possible.
2. Move it out your door as slowly as possible.
3. Pay as little for it as possible.
4. Save as much of it as possible.
5. Watch it as closely as possible.
6. Make sure more of it comes in than has to go out. That difference is called profit.
7. Know when to expect it and how much to expect.

If a small businessperson ignores any one of these rules, the result is hardship. Ignore two, it's trouble. Ignore three or more, and it's time to write a résumé and contact a headhunter.

To understand the significance of these basic rules, we need to discuss them individually.

Move It in Your Door As Quickly As Possible

During the good times, I became inattentive to the need for regular, timely invoicing of my clients. This had become such a deeply ingrained bad habit that it was difficult to break when economic times became leaner and meaner.

To correct this problem, I had to retrain our vendors to bill us more quickly, so we could generate our invoices on a tighter schedule.

Then, I had to make sure that our clients were paying us according to terms—full payment within thirty days. I knew I had some clients who weren't. In fact, my little company had become the "bank" for one of the wealthiest (and most overleveraged) individuals on the planet—a person with business interests in Australia, the United States, Canada, England, and several other countries.

Although there are a lot of nice people operating small businesses today, some people have told me that I may be too nice to be in business. I've always hated to go after the money that my clients owe me. I don't like being a bill collector. I have never stamped "Final Notice" on a monthly statement. I was almost embarrassed to ask clients for money. I rationalized that they wouldn't like to be bugged and that they would take their business elsewhere if I were to insist on payment.

To make matters worse, I have never employed a tough, aggressive person to do my dirty work for me.

Some of my clients figured this out and used the information to walk all over me. My attitude toward my receivables has cost me hundreds of thousands of dollars.

What folly! I finally realized that my receivables are *my money* due to me for services I had already performed and for a product I had already delivered. I had a perfect right to that cash.

If I didn't have my money, I couldn't use it to pay overhead, to reduce debt, to invest, or to save.

No matter whether the economy is in a boom or a recession, it's important to realize that there will always be customers who believe it is their right and privilege to use your money to operate their businesses.

You can use a number of simple techniques to move cash in your door as quickly as possible:

1. Insist on an up-front deposit as one of your conditions for doing business.

2. If you provide a service that will not be delivered immediately but for which you have an ongoing investment of time or materials, develop a plan of "progress billings."

3. State your terms of payment in advance, and make sure they are clear.

4. Follow up on your terms, and immediately go after the past due money.

5. If an account turns sour, turn it over for collection or pursue it through the courts without delay.

6. Avoid negotiating invoices with your customers or clients. Once you head down this path, it's difficult to turn back. Your customers will attempt to negotiate every invoice from that point forward.

As the result of bad experiences, I have a new resolve to bill quickly and to get on top of delinquent accounts immediately. My future depends on my ability to collect for services rendered. And because my current clients must bear part of the financial burden of bad accounts in the form of increased costs, I owe it to them to be diligent in the matter of receivables collection.

Move It Out Your Door As Slowly As Possible

The longer you can hang onto the cash that comes in your door, the more possible it will be to meet urgent demands and take advantage of exciting opportunities that may come your way. The goal should be to have sufficient cash on hand to meet at least the next couple of payrolls, to maintain healthy account balances to enhance your credit report, and to generate some interest income.

In reality, one of the perpetual problems with small business is that no matter how attentive you are to billing and collecting—to moving cash in your door as quickly as possible—there is never enough money to go around (unless you are fortunate enough to be operating a profitable cash-only business).

Thus, you may have to prioritize your bills and determine which ones get paid when. While yours may differ, I have my own list of priorities—one that has worked fairly well for over two decades:

1. *Payroll.* Without employees, you have no business. And no matter what great folks your employees are, if you miss a payroll they won't stick around.

2. *The government.* Withholding taxes collected from your employees is not your money. Don't *ever* treat it like it is. The governments—federal and state— want their money, and they want it *now*. The penalties and interest charges are too steep for you to consider using tax money as a viable form of short-term financing.

3. *Insurance.* This is your protection against disaster. If you don't pay your insurance company, it won't pay you when your building burns down, when an employee contracts a serious illness, or when your delivery van gets rear-ended.

4. *The phone company.* It takes just a few seconds for these folks to pull your plug.

5. *Other essential utilities.* Electricity, gas, and water are essential to running those computers, heaters, washrooms, and other basic aspects of office or factory life.

6. *Your most crucial vendors.* The suppliers you need the most deserve to be *at least* this close to the top of the list.

7. *Credit cards, leases, loan payments.* You can usually get a grace period on these items. After all, they'll just collect more interest from you, and interest charges are how they make their money. In many cases, they would actually prefer that you never pay off the principal. But remember, a good credit rating is vital to the future of your business, so do everything you can to protect it.

8. *Rent or mortgage payments.* It generally takes a long time for your mortgage holder to foreclose on a loan or for your landlord to turn you out on the street for default on a lease. For one thing, banks and institutional investors aren't interested in getting their property back. And landlords would rather get some kind of payment from you than have more empty space on their hands. As long as you convince them that you're doing everything you can to continue to pay your obligations, they'll usually work with you. In hard economic times, some landlords have willingly renegotiated leases midterm, to tremendous advantage for the tenant.

9. *Noncrucial suppliers.* These are the vendors you don't really need to stay in business. It hurts to say this, because I've been viewed from time to time as

one of those vendors. But we *are* talking priorities during those times when it's impossible to pay everyone on demand.

10. *Club dues.* Paying dues at private clubs is about the most nonessential thing you do with your money. And, now that club dues are not tax deductible expenses, people aren't exactly lining up to join them, and your club's management will usually work with you.

11. *Lawyers and accountants.* Hey, *they* make *you* wait! Just remember all those times you've called them and heard, "I'm sorry, he's in conference and can't take any calls" or, "I'm sorry, she's taking a deposition and will be tied up all day." (And I actually *like* my attorney and my CPA. It's simply that when it comes down to a question of whether I keep my phone service or pay my lawyer, I have no choice but to write the check to the phone company.)

Of course, the goal in prioritizing your payments must always be to keep your suppliers happy and preserve your credit rating.

One key I've discovered that enables me to keep my suppliers reasonably content with my payment schedules is to use as few vendors as practical.

There was a time in our business when we used up to eight photographers in a typical one-month period, to shoot product photos, models, ad layouts, brochure photos, and so on. The problem was, thirty days later they all wanted their money. And because some of the projects on which they had worked had not yet been billed and others had been invoiced to slow-paying clients, I didn't have adequate cash to meet their demands. Those we were less likely to use again right away had to wait for their money.

Now we use two or three photographers in a month's span. And we use the same ones on a continuing basis. We know that we can pay at least part of our outstanding debt before we ask them to do another job. They're happy, and we're living under a lot less pressure.

There is, however, an inherent and obvious risk in having too few established relationships with suppliers. If you rely on one key vendor in every category and haven't established backup relationships with others, you run the risk of being cut off, which, in the worst case, could effectively put you out of business.

It's crucial that you understand that I am not, under any circumstances, suggesting that you ignore your bills, drag out payments that you *could* make, create hardship for others, or stick the people to whom you owe money. I'm simply saying that you should hang on to your money as long as you can and that during times when you're cash poor, you should have a plan for assigning priorities to your payables.

Pay As Little For It As Possible

One of the stupidest things I've ever done is to finance some of my computers, video equipment, and office furnishings on credit cards. I have traditionally enjoyed a good credit rating and have signed a number of equipment lease deals at very favorable rates, but for some reason I took the easy way out and rang up massive charges on credit cards. So instead of paying 9, 11, or even 13 percent, I was paying 16.9, 18.8, 19.7, or even 21.3 percent on bank credit cards. (These are the same banks, by the way, that are paying 2.3 percent on savings accounts—at least at the time this is being written.)

In the future, I'm going to take advantage of some of the new lease options that make provisions for upgrades and that offer fund balances.

The lesson that I've learned is to research financing options so that I pay as little as possible for the money I borrow. It may take some extra effort to find the best rates or financing options, but over the long term, it's worth it.

I've had some positive experiences with loans that offer floating interest rates tied to the prime rate or some other factor. In the best plans (at least the best for predicting cash needs), the monthly payments always stay the same, but the term, or number of payments required, changes. My last airplane was financed for a seven-year term under such a plan, and immediately after I purchased it, interest rates began to slip. I ultimately paid off my loan in six years and four months.

Save As Much of It As Possible

I wish I could turn back time. I wish I could get my hands on all the money I've blown on pure foolishness over the years.

There was a time when making money in the advertising business was about as easy as growing weeds. In the late 1970s and early 1980s, despite double-digit inflation, double-digit interest rates, and nearly double-digit unemployment, the cash would just roll in.

I am completely embarrassed to tell you what I did with it. And I deserve to be. In addition to buying boats, airplanes, a company Mercedes, a corporate sports car, an office full of hand-crafted walnut desks and conference tables, and a stereo that could fill the Houston Astrodome with rich sounds, I *entertained*.

We were fortunate to have clients in both New York and Los Angeles—two great cities in which to entertain. To properly amuse our New York clients, my creative director and I would make reservations for the hottest play on Broadway, check into the Plaza hotel, book pretheater dinner reservations at Windows on the World, and then take a limo to the play. Following the show, it was a carriage ride through Central Park.

The Los Angeles client didn't require the same level of attention. But entertaining still involved an outstanding dinner at one of the great ocean-view restaurants in Malibu. You can only imagine how terrific I thought it was to finally get a client in San Francisco, the city of aftershocks, pretty bridges, and plentiful restaurants!

Things weren't too bad back in the Twin Cities, either. There were private clubs to join, new restaurants to try, and long business lunches to enjoy.

We threw lavish Christmas/Hanukkah parties in our office for our clients and suppliers, complete with live entertainment. The next day, it would be the staff's turn: overnight hotel rooms for everyone, limo to dinner, live music or perhaps a magician to entertain, and gifts and bonuses for all.

Meanwhile, the balances in our savings accounts, CDs, and investments stayed about even. That's because I wasn't saving, I was spending.

But did I learn anything through all this? It would not appear so. I noticed that we were doing so well near the end of 1991 that I decided to share our good fortune with one and all.

Our holiday office party for 200 or so of our closest friends featured two Renaissance-period musical acts, two live Santas, plenty of food and drink, and me in my brand new tuxedo. To draw this crowd, we mailed 500 videotapes of a special homespun musical number we called "The Christmas Wrap," which featured our staff "rapping" on camera to the beat of an original musical track.

The next night, it was the overnight in individual suites in a local hotel, the limo, and dinner for the staff in a beautiful Victorian mansion that some claim is haunted. Some people simply don't learn; I appear to be among them.

(In defense of our holiday festivities, I have to mention that two fine charities do benefit. We gather hundreds of toys for inner-city kids, as well as new clothing for both children and adults. And instead of giving our clients a fruitcake or a weekly planner or other present, we make a donation in their names to an organization that provides low-interest loans on quality housing to families who might not otherwise have a home of their own.)

The recent recession-driven hardships that have befallen my company have finally convinced me that saving and investing *must* become a priority. The company Mercedes and sports car have been replaced by a sensible vehicle with lower payments and reduced insurance and maintenance costs. The furniture will have to last several more years. And the holiday party has been stripped back to the basics.

My newfound interest in saving has raised a major question.

When I do manage to accumulate some cash, where should I put it?

I've lost enough in the stock market to know that I don't want to put it there. I know several people who make buckets of money in the stock market, but I doubt my ability to pick the right broker, the right stocks, and the right time to buy and sell them.

My other problem with investing in other companies—especially small to medium ones—is that I have no say in how they're run, where *they* invest my money, or how they will respond to changing technologies and changing markets. The world is moving fast, and I'm doing all I can to keep up with the changes in my industry, let alone anticipate those changes. I plan to take the conservative approach.

The key guideline I'm following is one I discovered in a book I have mentioned previously, Larry Burkett's *The Coming Economic Earthquake*. Burkett reminds us that we are becoming a global economy and advises us to diversify our investments through not only a variety of investment instruments but also through a wide range of economies.

As a result of his advice, my company and I now hold investments (limited though they are) in Pacific Rim mutual funds, European funds, conservative U.S. growth funds, certificates of deposit, a variety of IRAs, regular savings accounts (which are a joke these days, but at least they're highly liquid), and whole life insurance.

Many of my financially astute associates ridicule whole life insurance, pointing to the fact that term insurance provides essential protection when it is most needed (the early earning years) at a fraction of the cost of whole life. But, frankly, I don't buy insurance for protection alone. It is not my goal to make my children wealthy when I die. (Let them start their own businesses and make it on their own. The best gift my parents gave me was a sense of urgency about doing things for myself and the feelings of pride in accomplishment that resulted.)

My whole life policies are with one of the best-rated, most financially sound companies in the country. (They're solid because they don't own block after block of repossessed office buildings in every city in America.) If they go under, there probably won't be an economy to worry about.

The major advantages I've found in whole life insurance are: that the premium is predictable because it stays the same as I get older; the money I put in is returning 12 percent or better in dividends and paid up insurance; and, when I need quick cash, I have always been able to borrow it at 8 percent, even when interest rates were at their all-time high. On top of all that, I can pay back my loans on *my* schedule. If I don't pay them back at all, my loan balance simply reduces the face value of my policy. And when I retire, I can choose to take out my money in the form of an annuity, with a guarantee that payments to my survivors will continue for a minimum of ten years if I die within that period.

You probably have developed, or will develop, an investment strategy that puts mine to shame. I hope you do! But, above all, I hope you set aside a significant portion of your earnings in some form of savings program. There will be lean times ahead, and you will be in a better position to survive them if you plan for them during the good times.

Watch It As Closely As Possible

Throughout this book, I've bared my soul and pointed out the big mistakes I've made through the years, in the hope that you won't make the same ones.

Here's one of my biggest mistakes.

I haven't, until recently, watched my receivables. Something this simple just shouldn't be overlooked.

I haven't asked for cash up front from clients whose credit is doubtful. I haven't asked for credit applications, I haven't checked their Dun & Bradstreet reports, and I haven't moved quickly enough to collect when things turned sour.

Until recently, we seldom sent out monthly statements to follow up the original invoices. The nonsense economy has changed all that.

I now watch my receivables. I have my bookkeeper watch them. I have my accountant watch them. And we do more than watch. As discussed earlier, our new emphasis is on collecting.

But there are other aspects to watching your capital: watching your expenses, and watching your payables. The first of these will be covered in the point that follows, but the latter deserves attention here.

I once had an employee who didn't understand that ad agencies are supposed to bill clients for the gross amount and pay the media the net amount (which is 15 percent less). That's how we make a considerable portion of our money. This individual had a unique approach to the situation: bill the client for the net amount and pay the media the gross amount. It wasn't until a publication phoned us to ask why we were being so generous that we discovered the problem.

The point is, don't assume anything. Don't take it for granted that your outgoing invoices and payments are correct. Spot check them to make certain that clients are being billed the full amount and that suppliers are not being paid more than they deserve. Make sure that the amount they bill you is the same as their estimate, or the same as the number that appears on your purchase order.

In short, make sure that a competent person on your staff is checking, cross-checking, verifying, and reporting any discrepancies to you. And take the time to recheck for yourself from time to time.

Make Sure More of It Comes in Than Has to Go Out

One of the ways to make sure that more money comes in than has to go out is to watch your expenses carefully. That means watching your overhead.

The notion of "fixed overhead" is, in my experience, a myth. There is nothing fixed about my overhead. Parts of it may be fixed, but I'm not sure which parts they are. Health insurance premiums increase. The percentage on the employer's share of FICA goes up nearly every year. Employees are awarded raises. The cost of basic phone service climbs. Letterheads, business cards, and forms cost more every time we reprint them. That doesn't sound like "fixed overhead" to me.

What I *have* learned in more than two decades in business is that while my overhead isn't *fixed*, it can be *watched* and *controlled*.

In most businesses, the two biggest expenses are inventory and payroll. Depending on the business, one may outstrip the other dramatically. A book could be written on inventory control, and fortunately for you, several have been.

Although my business is based on people, ideas, and technology rather than inventory, I believe I have some observations worth noting.

The key to inventory is to meet the end demand, whether that demand is for quantity, timely delivery, or diversity. Where many companies go wrong is in not balancing those three factors. They get wrapped up with the "just in time" strategy to the point where one slip does them in. Or they adjust inventory based on today's sales and are unable to meet tomorrow's demand.

One of the worst cases of inventory management I've ever seen occurred in a small gift shop in an upscale specialty shopping mall in a Twin Cities suburb. This shop positioned itself as the source of the perfect gift for the person who has everything. Its shelves were stocked with the unique, novel, hard-to-find, high-tech gadgets that excite people like me.

I was so enthusiastic about the store that I pitched the owners to become a client of my ad agency. I had visions of this concept serving as the basis of a nationwide chain of franchises. And I'd be in on the ground floor. (In fact, someone did it a few years later. Ever heard of The Sharper Image?) Unfortunately for both of us, the management refused my offer. They believed their upscale location was enough to carry them.

As I continued to shop at this store, I noticed that its offerings were becoming less unique, less novel, less high tech—in fact, ordinary. The owners weren't seeking out new, exciting products, and they weren't stocking enough of what they did have. The shelves were becoming bare.

In the mid-1980s, my staff gave me a gift certificate for this store. When I went there to cash it in, I found that my favorite store—the one that used to be jammed with goodies I craved—didn't have one thing I wanted. I cashed in my gift certificate on something I didn't really want, because I guessed that the store would be out of business within a few months. And, sure enough, it was. In their misguided attempt to make sure that more cash came in than went out, the owners had depleted their inventory of the very things they needed to sell to remain in business.

The opposite approach also poses significant problems. A former client, a boat dealer, felt certain that the way to sell more boats was to make sure that the showroom floor and outdoor lot were jammed to capacity with new boats. This seemed to work when interest rates were low. But a little over a decade ago the rates ballooned, and he was suddenly faced with the high cost of financing his "floor plan." He obtained a second mortgage on his house to see him through. It didn't. His business succumbed to the heavy load of excessive interest costs.

To determine your cash needs, try to take into account the many changes that could occur—in interest rates, taxes, operating expenses, and the increased costs of raw materials or inventory. Have a strategy to deal with those changes if and when they occur, so that you're not caught short. Have cash in the bank, or be in a position to raise selected prices or reduce certain of your costs quickly. Make sure your relationship with your bank is healthy and secure. The worst time to go scouting for a new bank is when you need to.

Know When to Expect It and How Much to Expect

With a few short-term exceptions, my business has always looked good on paper. We have had substantial assets, significant receivables, and a healthy backlog of orders. At the same time, we've looked in the checking account and found that it was running on empty.

When that happens, we start looking at receivables to predict how sound they are and project when we can expect them to turn to cash. And just when we think we know the payment habits of a certain client, that client throws us a curve. Thirty days suddenly becomes ninety. As the inevitable result, our payables slow down, and our vendors get a little nervous.

Only recently have we begun to work with our accountants and financial advisers to do a regular cash flow analysis and projection. I can't believe we survived as long as we did without this information.

The bottom line—to use an overworked term—is that no matter how great your product or service is, no matter how timely your delivery is, no matter how professional your employees are, if you're not following the seven basic rules of capital, you're opening the door to almost certain disaster.

12

YOUR RELATIONSHIP WITH YOUR COMMUNITY

No matter what the size of your business there are tremendous rewards you can reap from caring about others. To paraphrase President Kennedy, "Ask not what your community can do for you; ask what you can do for your community."

Under federal tax law, corporations can give away up to 5 percent of their taxable profits. (They can actually give away as much as they want. They just can't take the excess as a tax deduction.) Five percent doesn't sound like much, but if every corporation were to follow this guideline, this nation would have much less poverty, substandard housing, and disease, and fewer hungry children.

We've become a nation of people who believe it is the government's responsibility to meet the desperate needs of our fellow citizens. Yet, the government has proven itself incapable of sound management decisions or of running any enterprise profitably. Private retirement plans work, but not Social Security. Federal Express makes a profit, but not the Postal Service. In fact, efficiency in the U.S. Postal Service has declined 19 percent in recent years as the result of the increase in the amount of time spent in "nonproductive activities."[9] And while the average postal worker with a high school education makes more than the average college-educated schoolteacher, the USPS continues to lobby for rate increases.

What, then, can we do to help our communities? To give back to the people who have helped us succeed in our business endeavors?

The avenues for service are almost endless and readily available. You don't have to do something on a grand scale. Begin with something small. Discover how great doing it makes you feel, and you'll be eager to do more.

What are some of the things we have done as a company?

Because we create print advertising and collateral material, we often donate our creative work to charitable organizations whose purposes we support. We have created brochures for a Twin Cities program that helps, counsels, and comforts children who are victims of sexual abuse. We have produced direct-mail pieces for an organization that places orphans from a variety of third world nations in loving homes.

To help others benefit from our experience in radio, television, and video production, we have created commercials and programs for the March of Dimes, the Minnesota AIDS Project, and the Children's Program of Northern Ireland, an organization that transports young kids from their strife-torn environment and places them in American homes for the summer months.

And, as mentioned previously, our annual Christmas/Hanukkah party benefits two worthy charities.

Through our involvement with the local Rotary Club, we volunteer to ring bells for the Salvation Army, we spend a day cleaning up a city park, and we sell roses to raise money to support the local food banks, provide a source of fresh water for impoverished villages in the Dominican Republic, and purchase coats, mittens, and scarves for disadvantaged schoolchildren in our community.

If none of these ideas appeal to you, here are some other things you could consider:

- You could sign up for the Adopt a Highway program, and you and your staff could keep a section of roadside adjacent to the highway free of litter. (In most cases, the name of your company appears on a sign along the stretch of road you maintain—an added public relations benefit.)
- You could plan visits to, and holiday programs for, people confined to long-term healthcare facilities in your area.
- Consider making provisions for time off work for employees who want to volunteer to lead Girl Scout or Boy Scout troops.
- Many communities have programs such as our local Meals on Wheels. They need drivers to deliver meals to the elderly or immobile people who are confined to their homes. Our area also offers a "Loaves and Fishes, Too" program that needs volunteers to cook and serve meals to the poor and homeless. Many churches and other groups sign up to serve one meal each week. And, as a side benefit, they develop an esprit d' corps among themselves that would be the envy of any company!

Every small-business owner should have a sufficiently developed environmental conscience to do the small things we all can do. Take the painless step of providing recycling containers for aluminum cans, glass bottles, and paper. Cancel multiple subscriptions to publications and route one or two copies throughout the office instead. Produce "rough" copies of your laser-printed documents on the backs of previously printed paper. Use recycled paper and packaging products whenever possible. And resist over-packaging the products you manufacture.

If you are a successful businessperson, you have a responsibility to give something back to your community—and our global community. And you have the opportunity to provide leadership to your employees, so that they can experience the rewards and self-esteem that result from service to others.

Don't base your decision on what you believe might be the eventual benefits to your company. Ask, rather, how your involvement will benefit your community and make it a better place for you and your employees to live.

PART THREE

Conquering Your Natural Enemies

13

BUSY-NESS AND BUSYBODIES

I'd pay a lot of money for days with more hours in them. The twenty-four each of us gets simply isn't enough to do everything that needs to be done. The demands of my business alone could consume all twenty-four hours.

But while I love my business, I don't want to spend every minute of every day enslaved by it. I strive to balance my time so that my wife and I can build our relationship; so my children can share their daily victories and defeats with a caring, involved father; so I can read, reflect, and learn during my few private moments; so I can enjoy the larger circle of family and friends; and so I can serve my community through my involvement in helping meet the needs of others.

I'm a committed believer in play, too. There's no harm in taking a break in a busy week to shoot a round of golf. There's no evil in spending an extra day off over the Fourth of July weekend. Your business won't be irreparably damaged if you work out at a health club three days a week, or take a Friday afternoon off to go boating or hiking with your family. In fact, your company may be better off as the result of the mind-cleansing qualities of play.

What all of this means in terms of my business is that I have to be as productive as possible during business hours. And if I am to achieve the goals I have set for my company, I have to ensure that my employees are as productive as possible, too.

This means taking control of the "great time wasters":

- Drive time
- The telephone
- The morning mail
- Meetings
- Systems and procedures
- Paperwork, reports, and memos

Drive Time

If you live in an area where traffic congestion turns your commute into a major time commitment (Los Angeles, for example), or if trips to other parts of your city are a routine part of your business day, you need to maximize your use of that otherwise minimally productive time.

One of your investments—if you haven't already made it—should be in a cellular telephone. This may seem like old news to most of you, but the fact is, fewer than 4 percent of American businesspeople have cellular phones in their cars or in their shirt pockets or purses.[10] I've had one since 1984.

When I offered phones to other members of my staff, I was met with skepticism. Some told me they thought cellular phones were a waste of money. I went ahead with my plans in spite of their objections. Today, they can't live without them. Travel time is now doubly productive. (Safety tip: Have the optional speaker and microphone installed so that you can keep your hands free for driving.)

Another great way to make your time in the car more productive is with audio cassettes. Many of the tapes I

listen to are on aviation topics, because I want to do everything possible to become a safer, more proficient pilot. But
I also listen to self-help tapes, including motivational gems
from the likes of Zig Ziglar and Denis Waitley.

I also carry a small tape recorder in the center console
or on the passenger seat, so that if I have an idea worth
remembering, I can get it down on tape. This alternative is
a lot quicker and safer than trying to fumble with paper
and pen to jot something down.

Through carpooling, if feasible, you can gain valuable
ideas and insights from other people. You can increase
your knowledge and understanding of world events, and,
occasionally, you can pick up a valuable business lead.

All-news radio stations and public radio provide up-
to-the-minute business news and often broadcast special
programs featuring interviews with, or speeches by, leaders in business, industry, and government.

Finally, there's no harm in using your drive time to
simply relax to good music.

It is better to find a way to make drive time beneficial
than to spend it uttering curses at all those "stupid drivers." I, for one, don't need to elevate my blood pressure.

The Telephone

The same guy who told you to buy a cellular phone is now
going to tell you that he hates telephones with a passion.
Nothing interrupts a great thought more effectively than a
phone call, and nothing irritates me more than a caller who
doesn't understand when the call should end. Add to that
the problem of "telephone tag" and you have the essence
of my frustration with Bell's most noteworthy invention.

I have a friend in the ad business who takes every call
without having any screened. That would drive me crazy.

Just the calls from the stock and commodity brokers who want to add me to their client lists, or the long-distance representatives who want me to switch to their service, would chew up the bulk of my day.

I rely on my receptionist to screen as many calls as possible. I prepared, and asked her to study, a list of the important people with whom we have significant relation-ships—clients, suppliers, prospects, and friends. If a caller isn't on that list, the call is handled by someone else and is referred to me only after all the details are known—name, position, company, phone number, and purpose of the call.

If I know I'm going to be in my car for an extended block of time, I have my receptionist take messages from all callers, with the promise that I will return the calls later. Then, on the way out the door, I grab the stack of messages and return them by cellular phone. When I leave the meet-ing or appointment, I call the office, pick up new messages, and return them by cellular on my trip back to the office. Sure, it's somewhat expensive, but in my business, time really is money.

Another effective habit to develop is to return all calls during specific "phone blocks." Set aside 10:30 to 11:00 A.M., for example, to return all morning calls, and 3:30 to 4:00 P.M. to return all late morning and afternoon calls. Incoming calls after 4:00 get returned the next morning.

Of course, if your business relies on incoming calls for sales, these techniques do not apply.

The Morning Mail

Every book or article I've ever read on office efficiency offers the same advice: "Handle each piece of paper only once. Answer it in writing, respond to it by phone, delegate it to someone else, file it, or throw it away. Whatever you do, do it immediately to reduce clutter and frustration."

Great advice. But I can no more follow it than I can flap my arms and expect to fly. My tendency is to sift through the pile of daily mail and look for the important stuff. *That* I respond to immediately. The less urgent items get placed in priority piles. Unfortunately, I have not yet learned to throw anything away, nor have I trained my assistant to do so.

Part of my problem with the daily mail is that, because my company creates direct-mail packages for some of our clients, I like to see what techniques other direct mailers are using.

Another problem is that, thanks to *Macworld* magazine and The Sharper Image, I have made it onto *everyone's* mailing list. I'm not exaggerating when I tell you that my mail is clogged with a minimum of twenty new specialty catalogs each week. Because these fine companies have gone to the trouble and expense to send me their literature, I feel morally compelled to read it all.

It gives me great pride to be able to report, however, that I am in recovery. I now recycle at least two-thirds of this bulk before I go home. I've also developed a series of prepackaged responses for a wide range of other mail, from résumés to requests for charitable contributions and free writing and design work. I now handle every piece of paper only *twice*. That's progress, believe it or not.

Meetings

Want to waste a lot of time? Have a lot of meetings.

Meetings can be one of the greatest threats to productivity faced by any business. My belief has long been that you can either hold meetings or do real work.

But some meetings are necessary. Among the valid purposes they can have are to

- Communicate information efficiently to everyone on your staff
- Obtain timely reports from employees
- Conduct interviews with job applicants
- Conduct job performance reviews
- Analyze procedures and develop strategies
- Solve a specific problem

You can use several methods to conduct more productive meetings and reduce the amount of wasted time.

First, set and adhere to a strict starting time. Don't let people hold up the meeting by wandering in whenever they feel like it. One of my former employees used to want to exhibit control and make a statement about how important he was by making his grand entrance several minutes after the rest of us were seated. After all, he must have reasoned, he was crucial to any discussion we might have, and, indeed, I was delaying the start of any discussions until he arrived and settled in. Eventually, I calculated how much productive time he was destroying, so I restated the need to begin meetings on time and began to do so. In subsequent meetings, we were well into our agenda by the time he arrived. He didn't like it, but he didn't change, either. For that reason and many others, he was one of the first to go during our downsizing.

Second, set and adhere to a strict stopping time. When a meeting lasts beyond its useful life, it becomes less productive and more of a social event. Make sure that when you have handled all old and new business, you end the meeting.

Third, limit the attendance at all meetings to only those people who need *to attend.* The larger the group, the more unwieldy it becomes. Employees shouldn't feel hurt if they're not included in a particular meeting. This is more of a problem in smaller companies than in medium to larger ones. At one time, I felt that I had to include everyone in every large-scale meeting to avoid hurt feelings. While I am still sensitive to the need to make everyone feel part of the team, we all do our best to limit the size of meetings, explaining that productivity is more important than meetings. If an employee can be doing his or her job instead of attending a meeting, that's what that employee should be doing.

Fourth, establish a set agenda in advance. Have a well-defined purpose for the meeting and know what topics you want to cover, as well as how much time you want to allow for each topic. In the advertising business—and possibly in your business—there is one notable exception: the free-wheeling, unstructured brainstorming session. Sometimes it's better to let wandering minds wander, especially when the goal is creative solutions.

Finally, keep an accurate record of who attended, what was discussed, who contributed to the discussions, and what was decided. This exercise has three functions: it will help you weed out unnecessary attendees, it will help you eliminate unnecessary or unproductive meetings, and it will help you follow through on decisions and individual or group assignments, so that you don't have to schedule another meeting to discuss the same topics.

Systems and Procedures

Some companies can be so bogged down in systems and procedures that they become immobilized. They let their operations manual dictate their every move, believing that to ignore procedures is to invite chaos.

As the owner of a business, you have a choice. You can do the work of busy-ness, or do the business of work. You can run your business, or you can let your systems run it for you.

Every company in these high-tech times seems to have a computer addict among the ranks. I made the mistake of letting ours set up some new, efficient office systems based on the latest time-saving software.

One program was supposed to make the relaying of phone messages and other interoffice communications more speedy and efficient. To me, it was annoying. Every time my computer beeped at me, I knew I had a message. I would have to switch from what I was doing to my electronic mailbox, retrieve my message, and, after I had read it, respond by electronic mail. Then, I would have to electronically discard it—a two-step process during which my computer asked me, "Are you really sure you want to throw this away?"

After months of frustration, I finally made an executive decision. I told my staff, "If you have a question for me, write it down, come see me in my office, or call me on the intercom. If there's a phone message for me, jot it down on one of those pink 'While You Were Out' slips." The minute I took myself off the interoffice electronic mail system, everyone else asked to do the same, because they disliked it as much as I did. The employee who set it up in the first place kept the program on his computer, but since there was no one else to talk to on the system, he eventually gave up.

Another great system was the reporting program that replaced my single job ticket with a series of printed records that broke out every conceivable component in every conceivable manner. Now, instead of having a single piece of paper that followed a job all the way through our company, we had to generate *six* pages of laser-printed paper for every job *EVERY DAY*. This not only tied up one of our laser printers most of the day, but it went a long way toward destroying our nation's forests. The demise of this system was another of my executive decisions.

Don't let systems take over your business. It will be difficult to regain control.

Paperwork, Reports, and Memos

Do you have memo writers on your staff? These are the people who feel the need to leave a paper trail covering every thought and deed. I don't know if they're frustrated would-be journalists, if they're trying to prove how much work they accomplish, or if they simply want backup in the unlikely event we ever end up in a courtroom face-off.

One of our clients tells the story of an employee who made certain that his brilliantly conceived memos were read by the boss. He would type up a memo, photocopy it twice, keep one copy for his files, and send the boss the original and one copy. Both would have the key points highlighted, and a yellow Post-it Note would be affixed, saying, "Please see the attached memo." He would then write a follow-up memo asking, "Did you receive my memo regarding such-and-such?"

If you must write memos, keep them brief and to the point. You don't need flowery language or detailed explanations. Instead, train the people who read your memos to ask you questions if there's something that they don't understand.

You will be able to gain mastery over the time wasters if you always remember this key point: The purpose of business is to create and sell a product, or provide a meaningful service, at a profit. If the activities you and your staff pursue on a daily basis do not contribute to that goal, they are nothing more than time wasters. They are busy-ness.

Busybodies

There's a good possibility that you have murderers on your staff. Cold-blooded, calculating killers. Their direct victim is time. Their indirect victim may be your company.

I wish I had all the time to kill that they do. But it's my company. I skip lunch to try to make it work. I come in early and leave late.

Do you have two (or more) employees who think it's their job to gossip? Is the coffee machine their most important business tool? Is lunch with each other the most meaningful part of the business day? Does your office telephone hold the key to success for their entire social life?

It's easy to let things slide, especially the things that involve confrontation and conflict. No one wants to get into an argument. No employer wants to "ruin" someone's life by laying them off, even if they're wasting time and not performing.

Fortunately for me, the three people on my staff who had "busybody-itis" left of their own accord. They've been replaced by people who really care about the company and want to see it succeed.

But when the busybodies were still a part of the company, they succeeded in irritating me beyond description. The reason was that I couldn't come up with a way to deal with them that didn't involve them getting angry, creating a stir, and compounding the problem.

For example, if an employee I wanted to see was on a personal phone call, I used to mouth the words, "Come see me when you're finished" and then walk away and wait for him or her to finish and get back to me. It occurred to me that this approach was wasting my time and that the message wasn't getting through.

I realize that people have an occasional need to make a personal call from the office, but they should have enough respect for me and the company to keep such calls to a minimum, keep them brief, or make them during breaks. The problem was that my employees' calls would last twenty minutes to a half hour each. Finally I concluded that if they couldn't control their calling habits, I would try to control them.

My initial solution was to stop by the person's desk first, indicate that I wanted to talk to him or her, then leave for one minute. Then I would return and stand at the offending person's desk until he or she decided to hang up. A few people considered this action to be an invasion of their privacy, but I viewed their phone calls to be an abuse of my time and a form of direct stealing from the company.

Then I hit on the ultimate solution. These people didn't have enough to do. I had to either find more meaningful work to occupy their workdays or to thin out the staff. No boss likes to lay off employees, but when profits are being squeezed by a recession, an early retirement or two could easily be the best decision.

Today, the busybodies are gone. I have a lean, aggressive, self-motivated staff that is too busy to waste time. They don't like to sit around doing nothing. What a refreshing change!

14

SLOPPINESS

When you first saw the word *sloppiness* as the heading for this chapter, you probably thought its content would focus on employees and the sloppy work habits that seem to prevail on the job today. Yes, we'll be getting to that matter in a few pages. But the best place to begin is with the boss—the entrepreneur who started the company.

The Sloppy Employer

During a recent meeting with one of my trusted friends and business counselors, he observed that my recent business problems should not have taken me by surprise. They have been, more or less a natural outcome.

Sure, some of the problems can be traced to the economy—to the deep and lengthy recession. But shouldn't I have planned for its inevitability? And, of course, some of the problems are the result of changing needs and changing technology. But shouldn't I have been more aware of them? Shouldn't I have expected and watched for them? After all, nothing in this world remains unchanged for long.

He observed, though, that my problems were precipitated by more than recession and change. They could be directly attributed to my own sloppiness. I had not minded my own store as attentively as I should have.

I had salespeople who weren't selling, and I didn't know it because I was not demanding follow-up reports. I was not adhering to the simple procedures that I had established.

I had an administrative assistant (one of the "busybodies") who was not administering mailing lists, filing systems, appointment calendars, data entries, or much of anything else, and I didn't know it. I simply assumed that because I was signing regular paychecks, the work was getting done.

I had a creative department that was losing job assignments (from our regular clients, no less) because they were preparing unrealistically high estimates for simple jobs. It could be argued that they were simply watching out for our bottom line, but all this happened during a time when we were reasonably profitable.

This is not to say that I had a lot of free time on my hands as the result of my inattention. *Someone* had to golf with clients and suppliers. *Someone* had to take the banker boating. *Someone* had to plan the social events for the Rotary Club. *Someone* had to sell hundreds of raffle tickets to raise money for worthwhile charities.

I had succeeded in setting the tone for the rest of the business. My employees were following my lead. "Things must certainly be great around here, because *someone's* sure taking it easy!"

It's humiliating to tell you how sloppy I had really become.

I would file tax returns on the last day—of the extension.

I would give employees their updated employee handbooks three months after they started with the company.

I would submit credit applications to vendors when I felt like it.

I would obtain credit applications from my clients in fewer than one out of ten cases. And I would never do an actual credit check.

I would insist on debt collection calls only after cash flow had become a critical problem.

I would listen to reports and updates from employees only when there wasn't something more urgent to consider.

These matters were not simply the result of procrastination. They compounded my problems simply because I did not realize how important they were. I was sloppy in my attention to, and execution of, my daily administrative responsibilities.

Do you now understand the statement I made in the Introduction, "I wish I could have been able to read my own book ten or fifteen years ago"?

If you've gotten this far in this book, you know that everything I've related to you is pretty simple. But, dear reader, mistakes are so easy to make. As a small businessperson, you have *so much* to do. Some things will simply have to wait. The key is to know what things can wait and what things need your immediate attention.

There are four things that need your immediate attention—four areas than cannot be the victims of your own sloppiness:

1. The needs of your employees, or interpersonal communications matters
2. The needs of your customers or clients
3. The need for cash
4. The need to cover your behind—legally, morally, financially

I addressed the first point in Chapter 9 ("Your Employees"), the second in Chapter 10 ("Your Customers and Vendors"), and the third in Chapter 11 ("Your Capital").

The fourth point deserves some discussion, because I have learned the hard way that sloppiness in this area will ultimately hurt your business.

Many business owners tend to procrastinate on some matters and skip over the details on others. The reasons are usually valid. After all, the basic needs of any business are to perform the tasks that directly affect productivity and produce income. There are, however, administrative tasks that cannot be overlooked. Here is my short list of must-dos. Consider it for your business.

- Make sure your insurance is up to date, that all potential perils are covered, and that everyone who should be enrolled on various health, disability, and life programs really is.

- If you require signed contracts from your employees (such as nondisclosure, noncompete, or general employment contracts), make sure they are signed before the employees' start dates, and that they are uniformly required of all employees.

- If you operate a service business, your contracts with your clients should also be in order, and if a matter comes up that may only get resolved in court, you should take action quickly.

- All forms and reports required by the government should be filed accurately and without delay. You should perform periodic checks to make sure you comply with all current regulations. Don't take it for granted that every employee or every department is automatically in compliance.

- Your sales tools should be up to date and readily available. You should never run out of forms, check blanks, letterheads, business cards, and other routine materials.

- Your inventory control system should be accurate and should provide for sufficient lead time for reordering.

If you are sloppy in any of these areas, there's a good chance your errors and omissions will be staring you in the face down the road. Ultimately, no business can afford sloppy management.

The Sloppy Employee

My downsizing and restructuring has had one very positive benefit. I now have teammates (or employees, if you prefer that term) who truly care about the business. My hope is that they see us succeed. They deserve it. They work long and hard. They give up lunches and vacations. They come in early and work weekends and holidays.

If you were to visit with them on the day this is being written, I'm sure they would tell you that the biggest discouragement they face is trying to correct the mistakes, oversights, and poor performance of their predecessors. When my new employees discover these problems, they realize that those who went before them didn't follow the basics of their job descriptions or adhere to the most elementary procedures. The sad truth is that I'm the one who let things slide into disarray.

There's absolutely no challenge to finding sloppy workers who don't produce. The challenge is in finding, hiring, and retaining the competent, detail-oriented employees you want and need, because every other company out there wants and needs them, too.

Sloppy workers can lose customers for the company, and correcting their mistakes can cost you huge sums of money. Their poor-quality work can even result in potentially life-threatening situations.

In our business we create and produce a significant number of printed pieces for our clients, including brochures, catalogs, annual reports, and direct-mail packages. Some of the larger projects cost $25,000, $50,000, or $100,000 or more, when all of the costs of writing, design, photography, and printing are totaled. A major error in one of these projects (for example, placing the pages in the wrong order) could lead to the client's rejection of the entire piece. We'd have to eat the costs of printing—often the major cost in the project.

To prevent errors and omissions, we have established an elaborate system of checks, cross-checks, and sign offs, which we call our "set in stone" procedures. This system has been quite effective, but invariably, when someone on our staff takes a shortcut (usually because it's a "simple job" that "doesn't require all those cross-checks"), a mistake slips through and we have to throw away the job. When an ad read "Prudential *Reality* Group" instead of "Prudential *Realty* Group," we had no choice but to rerun a corrected version of the ad at our expense. Fortunately, the client had a sense of humor, and we didn't lose the account as a result.

Sloppy work can even become a life-and-death matter, as I nearly discovered. My airplane was in the shop for a mandatory annual inspection and was returned with a clean bill of health. I was about to take it out for a flight when I decided to remove the cowling that covered the engine just to make sure that all the bolts, clamps, hoses, and wires appeared to be there, and in the right places. I discovered that the mechanic had left a screwdriver sitting on top of the engine. Had I not found it, it could have easily slipped into the path of the belt that drives the alternator. In flight, this could have precipitated a mechanical chain reaction that may have ended in disaster.

It's a simple fact of life that everyone makes mistakes. As the boss, it's your responsibility to make sure that systems are in place to both minimize mistakes and minimize the negative effect of the mistakes that do occur. It's also your responsibility to pay attention to your business— to make sure that you follow through on the hundreds of little details that are a daily part of a small business. Don't let poor work habits trigger the domino effect. There may be no way to stop the reaction once the first domino falls.

15

DEBT

I am convinced that the leading cause of insomnia, hypertension, and irritability among the ranks of most small-business owners is excessive debt.

That's not to say that debt isn't inevitable or necessary. No business that I know of can operate completely free of debt. Equipment has to be financed. Buildings require mortgages. And having an adequate inventory on hand usually requires borrowing.

But there are ways to control debt so that it doesn't control you. I've implemented some of these controls in my business almost from the start. Others I've discovered more recently, as the result of the ravages of the economy.

First, don't buy things you don't really need, until such time as you don't really need the money you'll have to spend on them. Invest in things that will make you money. Over the years, any time I had some "extra" money, I spent it on things that added no real value to my company. In other words, these acquisitions didn't increase my power to generate sales or income. Earlier, I mentioned my travel and entertainment habits, but that's just the so-called tip of the iceberg. I spent money on artwork, decorative antiques, mirrored walls, upgraded carpet and window treatments, and stereo systems for every employee's office, among other things. I should have been investing in computer backup drives, better software, and savings certificates.

Second—and this almost sounds contradictory—don't buy cheap things over and over. Buy quality the first time. I bought a top-quality leather executive chair in 1977, and I still sit in it for five or more hours every day. In contrast, I've done considerable bargain hunting and have purchased low-grade leather conference room chairs that haven't lasted two years. We usually *do* get what we pay for, and the cheap stuff has always proven to be just that—cheap.

Third, to make sure you don't get tired of the quality things you buy, avoid fads and trends. Buy traditional designs or clean, simple modern designs. Make sure the materials used are enduring natural products rather than trendy artificial substances that might look totally out of place in a year or two. If you walked into my office today, you would probably admire my desk without having any idea that it is a "modern" design over twenty years old.

Fourth, reread Chapter 11, on capital, and digest what I said about financing with high-interest credit cards. I'm convinced that bank cards were invented by the Devil himself.

Fifth, don't go into debt on fancy cars. All cars have three things in common: they break down, they depreciate, and eventually, they become old, ratty, and nearly worthless. Okay, I know. You need the flashy car for your image. That may be true, but let's be reasonable. Do you really gain more "image" by driving a $45,000 or $75,000 car than you would by motoring around in a $20,000 or $30,000 car? If it's that important to you, buy a clean used car of the make you want. Most people won't know the difference. Or care.

Sixth, sell equipment, furnishings, and other assets that you don't need as soon as it occurs to you that you don't need them. The longer you wait, the less these items will be worth. I had the good fortune of selling four computers that I didn't need about three months before the manufacturer offered a major price reduction on a similar replacement model. Had I waited, the prices on my used equipment would have dropped dramatically and instantly. I did wait too long on another piece of outdated equipment, and now I'm not even sure I can give it away. I've run numerous classified ads to sell it, with no response.

Seventh, use any new cash you generate (via the sale of equipment or other means) to reduce or eliminate the long-term debts on which you pay the highest interest rates. I realize that interest is a business deduction, but you have to earn the money to pay the interest to take the deduction. It costs you no matter what.

Eighth, refinance your long-term debt, and consolidate as much of it as you can at lower interest rates. You will have to run the numbers to make sure the bottom line works, but don't overlook this option. During the recent period of declining home mortgage interest rates, businesspeople were standing in line with the rest of America, refinancing their homes. Because I have every intention of staying in my current home for several more years, I jumped at the chance to lower my interest rate by $2\frac{1}{8}$ percent. After wrapping all of the closing costs into the new loan, I will come out "even" in less than two years, and gain after that. It was simply the smart thing to do. Yet many of the same businesspeople who jumped at the chance to refinance their homes continue to make payments on equipment and business loans at yesterday's interest rates.

The result of following these simple suggestions is that you will reduce your debt load, conserve future capital, sleep better at night, and be less crabby toward your employees, spouse, and children.

16

THE GOVERNMENT

It is hard to know what's more difficult, starting a business from virtually nothing and nurturing its initial growth, or keeping that business *in* business over the long term.

Through the evolution process that any business experiences, you will gain and lose customers or clients, hire and fire employees, watch as key employees seek opportunities elsewhere, and add and lose vendors or suppliers. In that process, you will make friends and create enemies. The fact that there will be people who do not like you or your company is indeed unfortunate, but it is true. Because I am a nice guy who likes to be liked, this reality cuts deeply.

One day, on an airplane flight, I amused myself by jotting down a list of those groups I thought were friends of my business and those I believed would prefer to see me go out of business. You may initially disagree with my observations, but upon further study and reflection, you may discover there's something to them:

The following people want me to remain in business:

1. Happy employees
2. Happy former employees
3. Landlord

4. Happy clients or customers
5. Creditors
6. Vendors

The following people don't really care whether I stay in business:

1. The government (state and federal)
2. Unhappy employees, although they need the job
3. Unhappy former employees
4. Unhappy clients or customers
5. Unhappy former clients/customers
6. Creditors with whom I may have had past disputes
7. Competitors

Most of the people who appear on either list are included for obvious reasons. But you may ask, why am I including the government at the top of my list of those who do not want me to stay in business? Before you conclude that I am some radical who wants to overthrow the government, I want to assure you that nothing could be further from the truth. I am an American who loves this country and my freedom. I just don't want to see the Berlin Wall rebuilt in America, either in reality, with concrete, brick, and steel, or symbolically, by a government with an insatiable lust for money (your money and my money) and power.

Today, while businesses in what were Communist countries are being returned to the hands of the people—to entrepreneurs with the desire to create competition in a new free market economy—the U.S. government seeks just the opposite. It seeks to regulate business, hobble the free market economy, and go into more businesses for itself. It gains the support of many Americans by convincing them that business has been irresponsible and that the needs of the workers, the poor, and the uninsured and underinsured can only be met through government intervention.

How Government Hurts Business

No matter how you look at it, the "governments"—federal, state, county, and local—simply are not the friends of business—small or large. What have they done to convince me that this is the fact?

First, government changes the rules in the middle of the game. True, some laws have "grandfather clauses" that protect those who have been operating under certain regulations and assumptions for a period of time. But basically, the government can change the rules any time it wants. In 1993, Congress voted to reduce business entertainment deductibility from 80 percent to 50 percent. Worse yet, they passed a higher tax rate that was retroactive to January 1993. Don't you wish *you* could somehow go back and get more money out of your customers after the fact?

When Jimmy Carter, our most vocal antiboating president, sold the presidential yacht, I knew I was in for trouble. Sure enough, shortly thereafter, in an attempt to "soak the rich," the tax laws were revised so that companies could no longer write off the expenses associated with the ownership of company boats. "Whine, whine, whine," you say. And yet my company boat enticed prospective clients, which translated into orders, which created jobs, which generated taxes, which paid our leaders so they could dream up more interesting laws and regulations.

Second, the government doesn't keep its promises. Take a close look at the so-called Paperwork Reduction Act. Have you noticed any reduction in the amount of paperwork you have to do to comply with government regulations? I can think of a dozen or more forms that have been added to my paperwork load since the Paperwork Reduction Act. That's the *net* increase in paperwork, so far.

Even if you haven't seen the direct implications of the Paperwork Reduction Act in your business, perhaps you've been through a number of home closings or refinancings. Since 1978 I have been directly involved in closings on three new homes, as well as three refinancings on those homes. In each case, the number of documents requiring our signatures increased by 15 to 20 percent. Most of these new forms were created by the government, not the mortgage companies, and they accomplished little more than to provide job security for the people who created them.

Third, the government doesn't always tell the truth. Take a look at the Tax Reform Laws of 1986. We were told that this tax reform would stimulate the economy, that it would be easier to compute taxes, that everyone would pay his or her fair share, and that, overall, that share would be lower. Instead, the laws created job security for accountants. And the economy has been uncertain ever since. Entire industries have nearly vanished, thanks to the latest "soak the rich" luxury taxes on such items as boats and aircraft. For example, in the late 1970s, general aviation aircraft builders in the United States delivered more than 17,000 new airplanes a year. In 1991 the companies that survived delivered only 1,100 new airplanes.[11] This dramatic decline is also partially due to skyrocketing product liability insurance and court defense costs—something else the government can't seem to get under control, even though several bills have been introduced in Congress that would provide substantial relief while still protecting the consumer.

Fourth, government is the lawyers' playground. According to former U.S. Senator Rudy Boschwitz of Minnesota, nearly two-thirds of senators who held office prior to the

1992 elections were trained lawyers.[12] The new Senate has about as many lawyers. Many of the rest of them are career politicians. Some are simply wealthy by virtue of inheritance, and a handful are educators or farmers/ranchers. The real problem for you and me is that there are very few members—probably only six or seven, according to Boschwitz—who are entrepreneurs or have any real experience in small business.

Both the Senate and the House of Representatives are out of touch with the needs and concerns of small business. As lawyers, they know how to write laws, so that other lawyers can argue over those laws, so that more lawyers who are now judges can make decisions based on legal precedence, which has been established based on how other lawyers argued cases before other judges, and how those judges decided those cases.

Fifth, our government is guilty of taxation without representation. The American Revolution was fought over this issue. Yet as a businessperson (in most states), you are paying unemployment taxes on your own income. If your business ultimately fails, your employees will be able to collect their benefits, but you will not.

Sixth, if you disagree with the government, the government wins. Okay, I realize that citizens have taken disputes with the government to court and have won. I don't happen to know any of them personally, but I've read about them somewhere. I have no desire to enter into discussions with the IRS about my business or personal tax returns. My goal, morally and ethically, is to keep them totally clean. Even though there are certain provisions I would like to fight, I can't afford to argue. They can.

Seventh, businesspeople do not achieve equal protection under the law. If you dissolve your business, the government has first claim—for any taxes you may owe, for the company, or for those withheld on behalf of your employees. That seems reasonable.

Next, you owe employees for any unpaid wages. That seems reasonable.

Then, you owe every other living human being on earth. That may be reasonable, ethical, and moral.

Guess who comes in last? You and your family. In times of recession or economic difficulty, you may be forced to defer some or all of your income in order to keep your company afloat. Then, if your business succumbs to the bad economy, everyone gets paid (insofar as possible) except you. The problem is that the government treats you differently. It recognizes everyone's claim against your company, except yours—the founder, the person who created jobs and opportunity for others.

In Chapter 9, I discussed ethics. You are probably going to think that I'm contradicting my own principles when I let you in on a secret you can use to give yourself a measure of equal protection under the law. It's called the security agreement, or UCC Filing. It only works if you are a corporation, if you have a board of directors, if that board determines your salary (and they're generous), and if you do not take out all of the amount they've approved. You have to be aware of the fact that the IRS does not look favorably on salaries that are out of line with the standards observed by other companies of your size within your industry. It views anything else as excessive compensation.

Dudley Ryan, our CPA and a lawyer, wrote in an article on excessive compensation, "For regular corporations, the IRS is taking a hard stand against entities that are 'deemed' to be paying too much in compensation. If this occurs, the IRS may disallow some of the compensation and recharacterize it as a nondeductible dividend."[13]

The article goes on to say that while there are wide ranges in compensation, the courts have found that several factors influence compensation, including

- The amount paid by similar size businesses in the same area to equally qualified persons for similar services
- The person's background and experience
- The person's knowledge of the business
- The size of the business
- The person's contribution to profit making
- The amount of time devoted by the person to the business
- The time of year when compensation is determined
- The nature of the person's duties

Assuming that you meet these tests and your compensation is not deemed excessive, here's how the scenario works. Essentially, you can protect the difference between the salary your board has approved and the amount you actually take out by filing a simple form, in most cases, with your secretary of state. Your financial interests can be secured by a portion of your company's assets and receivables, so that you have a place in line right behind the government and your employees—but ahead of your creditors.

Eighth, both the visible and hidden taxes on business are excessive. If you require leased office, retail, showroom, manufacturing, or warehouse space in which to set up and operate your business, your rent will include property taxes that are generally two to four times greater per square foot than the taxes you would pay on residential property. Why is this? Is your business using the school system? No, that's why you pay property taxes on your home. Does the high-rise office building in which you lease space require more police protection than the residential area four blocks away? Not really, because your landlord probably employs a private security service and has a better entry alarm system than most homes. How about fire department services? How many homes are fully sprinklered and have smoke detection systems that are set up to call the fire department? Many commercial buildings are required to have these features.

What the government doesn't seem to realize is that businesses do not actually pay taxes. Businesses pass their tax burden along to the consumer—or to their customer who eventually passes it to the consumer in the form of increased product or service cost. In every case, it is ultimately the end user who bears the burden of any tax. In reality, your business provides a disproportionate part of your community's tax revenues. You have become the reason why people want to buy homes in your community. You're helping to reduce their tax burden.

What You Can Do

If I've succeeded in convincing you that the government is not on your side, the logical question that follows is, "So what can we do about it?"

Sadly, not much. But three things come to mind.

The first is that you can help elect businesspeople to positions in local, state, and federal government. A pro-business Senate and House of Representatives would be a wonderful change. If you are able to identify a pro-business candidate, do more than vote for that person. Volunteer to work on the campaign. Drum up support from other businesspeople. Write supportive letters to the editor. Put a campaign sign on your lawn. Make a contribution to the war chest. We need people in public office at every level who understand our concerns and needs.

Second, you can join an organization that helps your voice be heard on Capitol Hill. There is strength in numbers—a single voice may be ignored by our lawmakers, but many voices speaking in unison cannot be dismissed so easily. I would suggest that you consider joining your local chamber of commerce as well as an organization such as the National Federation of Independent Business (NFIB). NFIB was established primarily to lobby on behalf of the concerns and interests of small business. For a modest annual membership fee, you are able to participate in regular membership surveys that define the organization's legislative priorities. You also receive a "report card" on the voting record of all senators and representatives on issues crucial to small business, as well as a nifty little magazine called *Independent Business*. (I've listed the address and phone number for NFIB's membership office in the appendix.)

The third thing you can do is avoid potential conflict by following procedures and policies to the letter of the law. I have seen business owners who have gotten into a disagreement with the government over some small point, and suddenly, every branch of government was all over them. (In some instances, the business owners *deserved* to have the government on their cases.)

Any accountant will tell you that once you've "flunked" a tax audit, no matter how small the error or omission, it is likely that you will be a perpetual target for audit. This can get to be quite expensive in terms of professional services and lost time.

One thing the IRS really watches for is the business owner who blurs the distinction between a legitimate business expenses and personal expenses. Personal use of a company automobile is one obvious area. Personal use of company credit cards is another. I don't so much as use a twenty-nine-cent stamp from the postage meter to mail a personal letter or bill without paying back my own company.

Another area that gets scrutinized is "travel and entertainment." The IRS does not want people to write off their vacations. I believe the safest way to play the game is to write off expenses only when a trip is 100 percent for business and has no personal component. That means that even though it worked out well for my board of directors to hold a meeting in southern California while my family and I were there on a vacation, I did not claim any business expenses or deductions for the trip. My view, however, may be more conservative than that of your accountant.

Whatever you do, place top priority on paying taxes on time, and file all forms and returns by the due date— unless you can afford to pay penalties and interest.

Government forms can really drive you nuts. They rarely make sense, the instructions are seldom clearly written, and there seem to be a number of different forms that all accomplish nearly the same objectives.

With the increasing number of forms I received, it finally occurred to me that I needed a better system for organizing them so that they wouldn't get lost in the shuffle of paperwork. I recently created a Government Forms file, and had my assistant set up a special calendar with "ticklers" to remind us when specific forms needed to be mailed. We always make a photocopy of every form we file, we make certain that our correspondence file is up to date, and we are doing our best to see to it that copies of everything are sent to our accountants.

The only way to get along with the government is to make certain that you dot every i and cross every t.

17

ADDICTION

Alcohol. Cocaine. Pills. These are the things that the word *addiction* brings to mind.

Chemical addictions are serious, true, and affect your company's ability to produce your product or provide service to your customers. But other, less visible, and equally insidious addictions can also harm your business. Addiction in any form is the enemy of business.

Workaholism

The most common addiction is *workaholism*. And the most common defense of workaholism is, "My company won't survive if I don't give it all I've got." Addictions, though, are often triggered by an avoidance mechanism. Excessive hours at work can often be used to avoid an unpleasant home life or other nonwork-related responsibilities. The office or shop becomes a comfort zone in which one can focus on a single set of problems rather than face the larger sphere of problems in one's life.

Workaholism can result from the belief that no one else can handle the job. Delegating is a fearful process. People *do* fail. In delegating, the real trick is to find employees whose failure rate is so low that a profit can be made in spite of those failures. Obviously, if the cumulative cost of an employee's mistakes exceeds the potential revenue that could be generated by the work tasks he or she performs, that employee is more of a liability than an asset and should be replaced.

No one ever intends to be a workaholic. The pressures of business sneak up on the owner, and slowly and imperceptibly, he or she goes into the office earlier and earlier and leaves later and later. The resulting devotion to work is not good for the owner's family, relationships, or health.

Workaholism is even more likely to become a problem in tough financial times, when it becomes increasingly difficult to stay afloat. You come to believe that the only way to improve your financial position is to put in those extra hours in the office, factory, or shop.

Technology Addiction

Technology addiction has recently become a problem for companies that use computers and other electronic marvels. It usually strikes the owner of the company, but in my case, as I've mentioned, it attacked one of my employees.

One of the problems directly associated with technology addiction is the learning curve associated with putting a new technology in place. You lose productivity because your employees are in training. Ultimately, the results could be positive, but try to evaluate in advance whether the proposed technology will ever compensate for the lost time and eventually pay for itself. For example, we made some software changes a few months ago that have yet to show a positive effect on productivity. In fact, even though the training cycle has been completed, the new system is more time consuming and generates more needless paper than the old system.

As owners, we often find ourselves paying our employees to learn new information that will likely change before they have assimilated it all. In our businesses, countless hours are lost to the learning demands of ever-changing technology.

Toy Addiction

Toy addiction seems to be reserved for business owners of the male gender. This is the one that got me. I am a marketer's dream—an early adopter. I want to be the first on my block to get the new this-or-that.

I was the one of the first people I knew to own an electronic calculator, way back in the early 1970s. It cost me $425. Now I can buy one that's smaller, performs more functions, doesn't require a huge AC adapter, has easier-to-read numbers, and costs a mere $3.99.

I paid $4,000 for my first Motorola portable cellular phone. Of course, I could use it the first day cellular service started in the Twin Cities. Now the new and improved model is $199 or less when a customer signs up for new service; and it's half the size and weight of the original.

When I bought my first compact disc player, it cost $400, and only a handful of titles were available, at $20 or more each. Today, some players are under $100, and the discs go on sale for under $10.

Toys can be cars, boats, airplanes, computers or innumerable kinds of gadgets. If their acquisition gets in the way of running an effective, productive, and profitable business, it's time to take another look at them.

Perfectionism

Perfectionism is an addiction that drives far too many owners of small businesses. In a previous chapter, I pointed out that while I don't believe in perfection, I believe in the *quest* for quality. I believe each of us should always strive to do a better job. The difficulty arises when the boss forgets that perfection will never become reality. Valuable employees can be driven from the company as the result of unrealistic expectations.

You have to accept the fact that people make mistakes. You will never find the perfect employee. Good management involves reducing the frequency of your workers' mistakes and controlling their negative impact on profitability. At our company, we operate under a simple philosophy: The more pairs of eyes that scrutinize a job, the better that job is likely to become, and the fewer the errors that are likely to be overlooked.

The Need for Acceptance

The longing for acceptance and recognition is an addiction with the hidden power to destroy a small business. Its most common symptom is the inability to say no. The boss accepts every request to head up charitable drives, serves as the chair of civic committees, prepares speeches for every worthwhile audience, and performs at least one good deed every day.

Usually, the motives can be rationalized: "A responsible businessperson has an obligation to give back to the community," or "It's great PR for the business." Good points. I believe in public relations, and I believe in giving back to the community. But I don't believe you should get so involved that your business suffers and your family doesn't remember what you look like. Don't let a healthy longing for acceptance and recognition become an addiction that controls you.

The list of addictions that could afflict the small businessperson is a long one. I know businesspeople who are sex addicts, compulsive gamblers, and even addicts of religious ritual.

It really doesn't matter whether the addiction is chemical, social, sexual, religious, or material, any compulsive behavior is likely to destroy you, as a businessperson, or your company—most likely both. If you, or someone who knows you intimately and cares about you becomes aware of a potential problem, your first step should be to seek professional help—quickly, courageously, and without embarrassment or hesitation. Don't let pride do you in. You're worth too much. Your family, your friends, your employees, and your customers all value you.

18

FEAR

Anyone who has ever been in business knows that running a company is fraught with turbulence, uncertainty, and pressure. Demands can, at times, seem overwhelming. Ultimately, every small businessperson is affected by the most dreaded of all emotions, fear. It is aroused by such questions as:

- Will my customers return again?
- Will my clients renew their contracts?
- Will I be able to make the next payroll?
- How will I pay my bills?
- What will happen if my key employees leave the company?
- Is my family doing okay in the midst of all my business concerns?
- What will be the result of this or that particular decision?
- What will I do for a living if my business fails?
- Will I be able to retire in comfort and security?

In a robust, growing economy, such fears can be sublimated with a certain degree of success. A recession, particularly a long and grueling one, provides a sharp contrast. Fear keeps the average business owner awake at

---

night. I know, because I have spent a lot of long hours in the fear closet.

I'm not an expert on the psychological implications of, or control of, fear. There are other books that explore the subject in depth. A few are listed in the appendix.

But I have learned four things about fear that have helped me better understand and deal with it.

The first is that *fear is common to all of us*. We all have our own favorite fears. The big, tough former head coach of the former Oakland Raiders, John Madden, I am told, is terrified of flying. He travels from city to city to fulfill his sports telecast assignments by motorcoach—a luxurious palace on wheels. I, on the other hand, who love flying my own plane, am afraid of climbing tall ladders. Some business owners I know are afraid of public speaking; others are afraid of water. What is one person's rational fear may seem completely irrational to another.

The fear that is shared by virtually everyone I know, though, is the fear of failure. None of us wants to be a flop. We want to be the brightest and the best in our chosen business ventures. Understanding that this fear is not uncommon is the first necessary step in dealing with it.

The second thing I've come to understand about fear is that *it is "just" an emotion*. It's not an irrefutable law of science or nature. It's not set in stone. That's why our fears change over time. We're not always afraid of the same things, because our fears change with both age and with circumstance.

The third point about fear is that *it's controllable*. The key to controlling it is understanding it. Why does this or that particular fear exist? For example, if John Madden understood flying—how airplanes work; why flying is truly the safest form of travel—he might conquer his fear of flying. Knowledge is power. (On the other hand, I am convinced that ladders will never be safe!)

If, as the result of the process of acquiring knowledge about a fear we are able to change the circumstances that surround it, we can control or eliminate it. If we are unable to change those circumstances, the fear will be an ongoing reality for us.

Here's an example. I have the fear that I will not be able to make my next payroll. My fear is based on the knowledge that I do not have enough money in my payroll account. Based on that knowledge, I realize that I must change my circumstances, first, for the short term, and ultimately, over the long term. Short-term changes could include borrowing from the bank, collecting a receivable, selling an asset, or cashing in a certificate of deposit. Long-term changes could include reducing overhead, raising prices or profit margins, increasing the speed of the billing cycle, cutting back on the size of the staff, or gaining wage concessions.

If I am unable to change any of the circumstances that led to the original problem, my fear of not meeting the next payroll will be an ongoing reality for me.

I'd like to be able to report that I am "fear free," but that is simply not the case. What I can report is that I refuse to allow my fears to control my life. If I did, I'd have shut the doors of my business years ago.

AFTERWORD
"I Love Ya, Tomorrow!"*

Most of you are probably familiar with the hit musical *Annie.* One inspirational scene in the play occurs when Annie sings the song "Tomorrow." Among the lyrics is this refrain, "Tomorrow, tomorrow, I love ya, tomorrow; you're only a day away!"*

The exciting thing about being in business, indeed, the exciting thing about life, is that we don't really know what tomorrow holds. So we can always dream. We can always hope.

You see, though many of my years in business have been tough, this past year has been devastating. But I am not devastated!

My family's standard of living has changed dramatically. Our savings—both corporate and personal—have evaporated for the most part. We've been faced with nagging illnesses, multiple surgeries, and huge medical bills. The company has lost significant pieces of business due to the economy, changing technology—and our own serious mistakes. We experienced a disastrous hard-drive crash

*TOMORROW from "Annie"
Lyric by Martin Charnin
Music by Charles Strouse
© 1977 EDWIN H. MORRIS & COMPANY, A Division of MPL Communications, Inc.
and CHARLES STROUSE PUBLICATIONS
All Rights Reserved. Used by Permission.

and spent thousands of dollars to rebuild lost files. We lost virtually all of our employees and had to train new people at considerable expense. It cost us over $48,000 in a recent ten-month period to correct the errors, oversights, and poor judgment calls of former employees.

To add insult to injury, two former coworkers established a competing ad agency and lured away three of our clients, in violation of the noncompete agreements they had signed without hesitation or objection.

And, of course, no story would be complete without an accident of some kind. We had ours on July 3, 1993, when—in the midst of a torrential downpour—another driver forced Karla off the road, into a light pole, and into a ditch with three feet of standing water. Her car was totaled, but, fortunately, her injuries were limited to two fractures in her leg, some cuts and abrasions from the shattering glass, and a lot of strained and sore muscles. Our four-and-a-half-year-old daughter, who was securely belted in the front passenger seat, escaped without injury. Her comment to me in the emergency room was simply, "Daddy, I don't want to do that again!"

When compared with the many years of business growth and so-called financial security we enjoyed, the past several months have not been easy for me to understand.

The first chapter of this book was probably all you needed to convince yourself that I was being driven by materialism. I'm certainly not going to tell you that there's something wrong with driving a nice car, owning a boat or airplane, furnishing your house with fine furniture, or carrying a Hartmann briefcase. I am telling you that I've had all those things, and they'll never replace family, friends, or peace of mind. I'm telling you that my priorities have changed.

Do I still want to own and operate a successful growing business? Yes.

Do I still have dreams to chase? Yes.

Do I still look with some envy at companies such as 3M and Microsoft, which were once small businesses and are now profitable industry giants? Of course.

Do I want success at the expense of my marriage and family? No.

Is the accumulation of money the reason for my existence? Absolutely not.

It's finally occurred to me that when one does have money, it should be used to enrich the lives of others to the greatest extent possible. As I go about the business of rebuilding my business, it is clear to me that I have a share of the responsibility for the poor, the hungry, the homeless, the elderly, and the ill. While I've always had a heart for the less fortunate, I haven't always done my full share. I'm the only one who can change that.

Am I going to be driven by fear? Not a chance.

Am I going to let anger toward the people who have let me down and have broken my trust destroy my peace of mind? No. People will always be people. I know they'll disappoint me from time to time. In facing the situation of my former employees who violated their contract and took away some of my clients, I realized that I had to practice what I preach. I could either be angry, and allow that anger to eat me alive, or I could forgive them for wronging me. I chose the latter, and wrote them a letter and told them they did not have to adhere to the terms of a court-ordered settlement and make payments to me for the business they were doing with my former clients. I never heard from them, but I know I did what was right. My anger has been erased— completely.

Ultimately, I had to ask myself this question: "Am I going to do my best under the circumstances?" No! I'm not going to let circumstances control my life. I'm going to do better than they allow. I'm going to live a positive, hopeful life, in spite of the circumstances, because I believe I have a positive, hopeful future!

I began this book in March of 1992. It took me almost two years to organize my thoughts and put them down on paper. I'm glad I did, because I have been one of the true beneficiaries of this process.

As I write this, I am fighting with every spark of energy I have—and with the help of a small but dedicated team—to rebuild our client base and pay off our old debts. On top of that, Karla and I have developed a new business concept that we believe will fill a real need in a meaningful way. We're putting together a plan to get it up and running.

As you read this, I want you to know that you can be certain of some things in life (in addition to death and taxes). You can be certain that operating a small business will always be a great adventure—because you will always confront the unexpected. That's exciting, and it's one of the many things that makes being an entrepreneur so appealing to me.

You can also be certain that the economy will always have its peaks and valleys, and that the changing economic environment will affect every business to some extent. As a businessperson, you will always have to adapt to change, and perhaps rethink and redirect your dream.

You can count on technology to change, too. Just as the computer revolution affected my advertising business by enabling some of my clients to do their work in-house, there are other—now unimaginable—technological changes ahead. Be alert to the changes that could affect your industry and your business, and consider your possible responses carefully. Seek the advice of others, as well.

You can also be assured that you and I, if we are true entrepreneurs, will never be satisfied reporting to someone else. We will find a way to be in business for ourselves. We will create our own opportunities. We will remain positive, hopeful, and energetic. We will anticipate tomorrow with eagerness.

And we will use every bit of common sense we possess to win every new battle with the nonsense economy!

Appendix A

The Ten Best Things About Being in Business for Myself

1. I own my own desk and chair.
2. I have the authority to hire good people.
3. I have the authority to fire unproductive people.
4. I can distribute my profits any way I want—as bonuses to myself, to my staff, or as charitable contributions.
5. I can take long lunches.
6. When times are good, I sleep like a baby.
7. I can come in late in the morning, and no one will yell at me.
8. I can take the afternoon off to go golfing or boating, without asking permission.
9. I get a feeling of accomplishment knowing that I am building a business that may live on after I am gone.
10. I have the opportunity to build equity through my own work, and the work of my employees.

The Ten Worst Things About Being in Business for Myself

1. I have to pay for all of the desks and chairs.

2. I have to fire jerks who want to get even with me, and sometimes I have to lay off really good, dedicated people.

3. I occasionally have to pay unemployment benefits for people who weren't doing their jobs.

4. My rent or mortgage will always drain too much cash, mostly thanks to disproportionately high taxes on commercial property.

5. I always have to deal with other people's lawyers.

6. When times are bad, I have difficulty sleeping.

7. If I go under, I won't be able to collect unemployment, even though I've had to pay into it based on my salary.

8. I very seldom have the time to take off an afternoon to go golfing or boating—at least lately.

9. I never really get to go on vacation. Even when I try to hide out for a week in Aruba, I have to call the office to find out if enough cash came in to cover the checks I signed before I left.

10. I have to cope with insurance agents, accountants, IRS agents, and more government agencies than I can count.

APPENDIX B

The Ten Best Things About Working for Someone Else

1. You don't have to pay for your own desk and chair.
2. Unless you're a manager, you don't have to make decisions about hiring or firing.
3. You'll never know the pain of laying off a good employee— simply because of budget cutbacks.
4. You don't have to pay the rent.
5. You don't have to deal with lawyers—unless that's in your job description.
6. If you lose your job, you'll be able to collect unemployment.
7. When you go on vacation, chances are you can completely forget about your job and enjoy yourself.
8. You don't have to pay the interest on the money your employer borrows.
9. You probably sleep better at night than I do.
10. You don't have to cope with insurance agents, accountants, IRS agents, and more government agencies than you can count.

The Ten Worst Things About Working for Someone Else

1. You don't own your own desk and chair.
2. Unless you're a manager, you can't hire good people and fire the jerks.
3. You have little or no role in determining your raises, benefits, and bonuses.
4. You have little control over the work environment.
5. You have no say in how profits are distributed.
6. When times are bad, you realize you could get laid off, and you have difficulty sleeping.
7. You have to arrive at work on time and confine your lunches to one hour.
8. You can't go golfing whenever you want.
9. You are not the final authority on company policy, although in a progressive company, your opinions will be heard.
10. You can't hire or fire your boss.

APPENDIX C

Computer Operational Guidelines

One of the biggest single disasters we have faced in our business to date was the "hard" crash of a large-capacity hard drive. ("Hard" means that all data— software, documents, type fonts, everything—was lost in the crash.) This hard drive was poorly backed up (less than 50 percent) and the cost of recreating the documents, at our expense, was mammoth.

Fortunately, we all learn from our mistakes. Our immediate response was to set up a series of guidelines for the naming, maintenance, and backing up of files, along with a way to verify, on a daily basis, that the procedures were being followed.

These policies are designed for companies using desktop or laptop computers and assume that the computers are linked by a local area network (LAN). They can be modified and applied to suit the needs of companies that use PC's/Macs without LAN's or those that utilize mainframe and workstations, as well. The policies should be written, published, and included in employee handbooks or training manuals.

Here is a summary of our policies, which you are free to reproduce and modify as you choose.

The following computer policies, procedures, and operational guidelines will be followed by all members of our team, *without exception.*

1. All new work will be backed up daily to another format. It is the responsibility of each person to back up their own material either on floppy disk or cartridge drive.

2. All backups must be clearly organized, labeled, and must be easily and quickly located.

3. Every two weeks (on paydays), the entire contents of all hard drives will be backed up to DAT (Digital Audio Tape), and the DAT copy will be stored off-site in the company's safe-deposit box. The designated person will handle this procedure, and will train another party to handle the procedure in his or her absence.

4. There will be no encrypting, coding, or password protection of any files without your supervisor's permission. Any passwords used to lock files must be known by the supervisor and cannot be changed without notifying her or him first.

5. All files and documents must have clear, concise names, so that other persons can locate and identify files during the absence of the person who originally created the file. (Generally, the Job Number, followed by a Version or Revision Number, will be the accepted way of identifying files.) "Cute" names, or names which mean something only to the file creator, will not be used.

6. Hard disks and file servers will not have cute or meaningless names. The employee's name or initials (or department name) will be used to identify all hard drives and published files.

7. Neither the system folder nor any other folders, icons, or programs will be hidden. The finder must display all folders that have been created, and the contents of each folder must appear when called up. (This means we have an open desktop policy.)

8. The company does not authorize or permit the copying of software except for the purpose of creating a backup copy of original program disks, nor does it permit the distribution of software for which we do not hold licenses.

9. Software and software documentation (manuals) are not to be removed from the office for any purpose whatsoever.

10. The latest version of our virus protection program must be installed on all computers, and the entire hard drive must be examined upon installation of the new version. Every computer must be programmed to allow this software to examine all diskettes automatically upon mounting. All new programs or files obtained from outside sources must be examined before use. Suspect software or documents that cannot be diagnosed and repaired by the virus protection program must not be used.

11. New programs cannot be installed on any computers without permission.

12. Games, screensavers, and sounds cannot consume more than 5 percent of the space on any hard drive.

13. Per the policies contained in the employee handbook, company computers are not to be used for personal purposes or for freelance work, whether it is pro bono or for compensation or barter.

Appendix D

Business Consulting Organizations

ACME—The Association of Management Consulting Firms
521 Fifth Avenue, 35th Floor, New York, NY 10175
Phone: (212) 697-9693, Fax: (212) 949-6571

American Association of Healthcare Consultants
11208 Wapels Mill Road, Suite 109, Fairfax, VA 22030
Phone: (703) 691-2242, Fax: (703) 691-2247

American Consultants League
1290 North Palm Avenue, Suite 112, Sarasota, FL 34236
Phone: (813) 952-9290, Fax: (813) 925-3670

American Consulting Engineers Council
1015 15th Street, N.W., Suite 802, Washington, DC 20005
Phone: (202) 347-7474, Fax: (202) 898-0068

Association of Consulting Chemists and Chemical Engineers
Chemist's Club, 40 W. 45th Street, New York, NY 10036
Phone: (212) 983-3160, Fax: (212) 983-3161

Association of Executive Search Consultants
230 Park Avenue, Suite 1549, New York, NY 10169
Phone: (212) 949-9556, Fax: (212) 949-9560

Association of Internal Management Consultants
P.O. Box 304, East Bloomfield, NY 14443
Phone: (716) 657-7878, Fax: (716) 657-6070

Association of Productivity Specialists
200 Park Avenue, Suite 303E, New York, NY 10017
Phone: (212) 286-0943

Council of Consulting Organizations
521 Fifth Avenue, 35th Floor, New York, NY 10175
Phone: (212) 697-9693, Fax: (212) 949-6571

Financial Executives Institute
10 Madison Avenue, P.O. Box 1938, Morristown, NJ 07962-1938
Phone: (201) 898-4600, Fax: (201) 898-4649

Franchise Consultants International Association
5147 South Angela Road, Memphis, TN 38117
Phone: (901) 682-2951, Fax: (901) 685-5282

Independent Computer Consultants Association
933 Gardenview Office Parkway, St. Louis, MO 63141
Phone: (314) 997-4633, Fax: (314) 567-5133

Institute of Management Consultants
521 Fifth Avenue, 35th Floor, New York, NY 10175
Phone: (212) 697-9693, Fax: (212) 949-6571

International Association of Merger and Acquisition
Consultants
60 Revere Drive, Suite 500, Northbrook, IL 60062
Phone: (708) 323-0233, Fax: (708) 480-9282

National Association of Export Companies
P.O. Box 1330, Murray Hill Station, New York, NY 10156
Phone: (212) 725-3311, Fax: (212) 725-3312

National Association of Personal Financial Advisors
1130 W. Lake Cook, Suite 150, Buffalo Grove, IL 60089-1974
Phone: (708) 537-7722, Fax: (708) 537-7740

Professional and Technical Consultants Association
(Membership concentrated in Northern California)
P.O. Box 4143, Mountain View, CA 94040
Phone: (415) 903-8305, Fax: (415) 967-0995

Public Relations Society of America
33 Irving Place, 3rd Floor, New York, NY 10003-2376
Phone: (212) 995-2230, Fax: (212) 995-0757

For information on membership in the National Federation of
Independent Business, write to:

National Federation of Independent Business
53 Century Boulevard, Suite 300, Nashville, TN 37214
Phone: (615) 872-5800, Fax: (615) 872-5899

RECOMMENDED READING

Bell, Donald L. *Minding Other People's Business: Winning Big for Your Clients and Yourself.* New York: Villard Books, 1989.

Blanchard, Kenneth, and Spencer Johnson. *The One-Minute Manager: Increase Productivity, Profits, and Your Own Prosperity.* New York: Morrow, 1982.

Blanchard, Kenneth, and Norman Vincent Peale. *The Power of Ethical Management.* New York: Morrow, 1988.

Brown, W. Steven. *13 Fatal Errors Managers Make: And How You Can Avoid Them.* Old Tappan, N.J.: Revell, 1985.

Burkett, Larry. *Business by the Book: The Complete Guide of Biblical Principles for Business Men and Women.* Nashville: Thomas Nelson Publishers, 1990.

Burkett, Larry. *The Coming Economic Earthquake.* Chicago: Moody Press, 1991.

Colson, Chuck, and Jack Eckerd. *Why America Doesn't Work: How the Decline of the Work Ethic Is Hurting Your Family and Future—And What You Can Do.* Dallas: Word Publishing, 1991.

Connor, Richard A., Jr., and Jeffrey P. Davidson. *Getting New Clients.* New York: John Wiley & Sons, 1987.

Covey, Stephen R. *Principle-Centered Leadership.* New York: Fireside, 1992.

—. *The Seven Habits of Highly Effective People.* Hamden, Conn.: Fireside, 1990.

Daniels, Peter J. *How to Be Happy Though Rich.* Old Tappan, N.J.: Revell, 1984.

Della Femina, Jerry. *From Those Wonderful Folks Who Gave You Pearl Harbor: Front-line Dispatches from the Advertising War*. New York: Pocket Books, 1971.

Drucker, Peter F. *The Effective Executive*. New York: Harper, 1966.

Fulghum, Robert. *All I Needed to Know I Learned in Kindergarten: Uncommon Thoughts on Common Things*. New York: Villard Books, 1989.

Glennon, Jim. *Your Healing Is Within You*. South Plainfield, N.J.: Bridge Publishing, 1980.

Handly, Robert, with Pauline Neff. *Anxiety and Panic Attacks: Their Cause and Cure*. New York: Fawcett, 1987.

Iacocca, Lee, with William Novak. *Iacocca: An Autobiography*. New York: Bantam, 1986.

Iacocca, Lee, with Sonny Kleinfield. *Talking Straight*. New York: Bantam, 1988.

Larson. Bruce. *Living Beyond Our Fears: Discovering Life When You're Scared to Death*. San Francisco: Harper, 1990.

LeBoeuf, Michael. *How to Win New Customers and Keep Them for Life*. New York: Berkley Books, 1985.

Lele, Milind M., with Jagdish N. Sheth. *The Customer is Key: Gaining an Unbeatable Advantage Through Customer Satisfaction*. New York: John Wiley & Sons, 1987.

Mackay, Harvey. *Beware the Naked Man Who Offers You His Shirt: Do What You Love, Love What You Do, and Deliver More than You Promise*. New York: Morrow, 1990.

—. *How to Swim with the Sharks Without Being Eaten Alive: Outsell, Outmanage, Outmotivate and Outnegotiate Your Competition*. New York: Morrow, 1988.

McCormick, Mark H. *What They Don't Teach You at Harvard Business School: Notes from a Street-Smart Executive*. New York: Bantam, 1984.

Noble, Sara P., ed. *301 Great Management Ideas from America's Most Innovative Small Companies*. Boston: INC. Magazine, 1991.

Ogilvy, David. *Ogilvy on Advertising*. New York: Random House, 1985.

Peale, Norman Vincent. *Positive Imaging: The Powerful Way to Change Your Life*. New York: Fawcett Crest, 1985.

Peters, Thomas H., and Robert H. Waterman, Jr. *In Search of Excellence: Lessons from America's Best-Run Companies*. New York: Warner Books, 1983.

Ringer, Robert J. *Million Dollar Habits*. New York: Fawcett Crest, 1990.

Roberts, Wes. *Leadership Secrets of Attila the Hun*. New York: Warner Books, 1985.

Sewell, Carl, and Paul B. Brown. *Customers for Life: How to Turn That One-Time Buyer into a Lifetime Customer*. New York: Pocket Books, 1990.

Valles, Carlos G. *Letting Go of Fear: Tackling Our Worst Emotion*. New York: Triumph Books, 1991.

Waitley, Denis. *Seeds of Greatness: The Ten Best Kept Secrets of Total Success*. Old Tappan, N.J.: Revell, 1988.

Waterman, Robert H., Jr. *The Renewal Factor: How the Best Get and Keep the Competitive Edge*. New York: Bantam, 1987.

Ziglar, Zig. *Zig Ziglar's Secrets of Closing the Sale*. New York: Berkley, 1987.

ENDNOTES

Chapter 1

1. Larry Burkett, *The Coming Economic Earthquake* (Chicago: Moody Press, 1991).

Chapter 2

2. Mitchell Pacelle, "Noted Architect's Firm Falls Apart in Fight Over Control, Clients," *Wall Street Journal*, September 2, 1992, p. 1.

Chapter 4

3. Laurence J. Peter, *The Peter Principle* (New York: Morrow, 1974).

Chapter 7

4. "Major Overhaul," *Time*, December 30, 1992, p. 56.

Chapter 8

5. Peter J. Daniels, *How to Be Happy Though Rich* (Old Tappan, N.J.: Revell, 1984).

Chapter 9

6. Isabel Wilkerson, "Once an Owner, Now Glad to Scrub Toliets," *Minneapolis Star-Tribune*, March 8, 1992, p. 15A.

Chapter 10

7. Michael LeBoeuf, *How to Win Customers and Keep Them for Life* (New York: Berkley, 1989).

8. Carl Sewell and Paul B. Brown, *Customers for Life* (New York: Pocket Books, 1991).

Chapter 12

9. Charles Colson and Jack Eckerd, *Why America Doesn't Work* (Dallas: Word Publishing, 1991), p. 25.

Chapter 13

10. *Standard & Poors Industry Surveys*, October 1992 (New York: Standard & Poors, 1992).

Chapter 16

11. Phil Boyer, "President's Position," *AOPA PILOT*, December 1992 (citing statistics provided by the General Aviation Manufacturers Association).

12. At my request, former U.S. Senator Rudy Boschwitz performed a line-by-line review of the U.S. Senate roster, to substantiate his long-standing claim that most senators are lawyers and few have any experience or background in business.

13. Dudley Ryan, "IRS Attacking Compensation Levels," *The LAWCO Report*, September 1992, p. 5.

INDEX